Half-Breed Runaway

Elizabeth P. Brown

ELECTIO PUBLISHING
first century principles.
a twenty-first century approach.

Half-Breed Runaway
By Elizabeth P. Brown

Copyright 2018 by Elizabeth P. Brown. All rights reserved.
Cover Design by eLectio Publishing

ISBN-13: 978-1-63213-518-6

Published by eLectio Publishing, LLC

Little Elm, Texas

http://www.eLectioPublishing.com

5 4 3 2 1 eLP 22 21 20 19 18

Printed in the United States of America.

The eLectio Publishing creative team is comprised of: Kaitlyn Campbell, Emily Certain, Lori Draft, Jim Eccles, Sheldon James, and Christine LePorte.

Publisher's Note

The publisher does not have any control over and does not assume any responsibility for author or third-party websites or their content.

Contents

Acknowledgments

T his book of labor in love and obedience to God my Father in Heaven, the source of my strength and well of love, began 12 years ago. "I love you, O' Lord, my strength" Psalms 18:1. Having the time to write while I worked as a full time (and overtime) social worker, go to school for my Master's, study and earn my clinical license while raising three boys, was beyond me. But, God always makes a way for his purpose and there were plenty of times I was a reluctant writer as the subject still stings me with pain.

At this stage of my life, there are many who have made an impact during my journey and although nameless in this part, I thank you.

To my mother, Zeniada whose love and strength lifted my heart and spirit during my darkest hours. My brother Ronnie who was the perfect, protective big brother. I am thankful and blessed for my loving boys, Leonice Jr., Xavier and Justice who make parenting a joy. I love you and it's an honor to be your mother. When friends ask, "What did you do? What's your secret?", I said I prayed and still do every day.

Jennifer Silva Redmond, my literary coach and editor, a precious gem with mounds of patience who deserves many thanks as her advice encouraged me to keep writing and find a publisher because she believed the story needed to be heard by a greater population. Were it not for her, I would have self-published and hid comfortably, but alas, God led me to Jennifer who kept this journey going.

Erika, my best friend who knows me more than I know myself. Thank you for spoon feeding me through rough days when I didn't want to eat, and calling me to provide comfort when you feel my pain.

I miss my grandmother, Elizabeth, and watch one of her favorite TV show every night in remembrance of her love and forever grateful that she wouldn't allow my father to forget me in the Philippines. I'm thankful to my uncle who took me in and showed me love as a heaven-sent earthly father does; my aunt whose strength inspired me and cousin who made my days full of fun and surprises.

Thank you to my special friends, Andrea and Ms. Ella for showing me the love of a mother by how you treat me and your own.

My brothers, sisters and sister-in-law whose love and adoration kept me connected with family, especially CJ who is my champion and keeps me on a short leash so that I can't stray too far. To my father for bringing me to the land where dreams come true and my stepmother for showing love to my boys.

I thank my publishing company for the opportunity to work together.

I give thanks to my church Pastor Ken Hart of The Highlands Christian Fellowship who reminds us to be influencers and to make an impact in this world according to our God-given talents.

To the love of my life and companion, although faceless, the promise of you was enough to keep me pushing through during tough times.

To those experiencing abuse and/or neglect, I pray for you. May God's love, grace and mercy find and carry you today and every day even more than he did for me.

To those who are reading my book, thank you for your time and please help someone in need.

Where Do I Begin?

I am Elizabeth, Eliza for short, Eli for even shorter, and I'm ten years old. It's Saturday, so school's out—a good day to run away. I didn't need an alarm clock to wake up, I couldn't sleep. The clock showed five. Thump-thump, thump-thump, my heart raced inside my chest.

"Please, God, help me," I whispered, hands clasped together on my knees by my bedside. I stood up. The stillness amplified my heartbeat so it sounded like thunder. I squinted, trying to see in the dark since I couldn't use the light. I'd set out everything in place last night. I reached for *my* dress, the one Mom gave me for the special occasion of meeting my new family—a white polka-dot dress with a purple bow at the neckline. A pair of white socks with lace trim and black shoes with bows on top completed it. Mom bought it at the market; I was thrilled to have something new. Any other day, she would say we couldn't afford it, but that day, we splurged. I didn't ask any questions, distracted by the beauty, the colors, and the new stuff smell. Now, I would much prefer the tattered clothing I used to wear.

A tear dropped onto my lap and jolted me back to reality. No time to waste. I put on my dress, with little noise and only a small whimper. It had been a year—my dress was a bit short and tight, but it'd have to do. I didn't want Ms. Ama to call the police and say I had stolen things. She told me that if they sent me back to Mom, I wouldn't be able to take anything with me. I didn't care about the clothes she bought, the doll they gave me, or the mounds of food I ate. They all came at a high price.

I slipped on my shoes which perfectly fit from heel to toe, with no more room to give. I was going to be a ghost—not even a memory in their lives. I wished I was leaving the same person I came as, but my heart and spirit were irreparably crushed.

Everyone was still asleep. The house was perfectly quiet. It would be that way until about 8 a.m. and then cleaning time—at least it would have been for me. *I'll be long gone by then. I can't get caught.*

I opened my door. No one was in the hallway. I tiptoed across the kitchen, praying that the shiny wooden floors wouldn't creak and tell on me as I headed toward the back door. I was fired up and scared at the same time, my heart pumping wildly, ready to jump out of my chest. The rest of me was smooth and steady. Every step became easier. I opened the back door, my willing quiet accomplice, squeezed out, and closed it slowly. I was out. *No turning back now.* It was still dark outside, but there was enough light to see my way. It was peaceful and quiet, smelling of fresh dew. I started to run. It was easy with nothing to carry; everything I owned was a light load.

I had memorized my friend Cindy's address and passed by it a few times on my way home from school. She invited me to visit anytime so hopefully they were ready for me. My mind raced, creating fantasies of my new beginning with a new family, just like when I left my mom and went to live with my father.

The sun began to light up the world, making clear my path. I reached my destination, but I didn't see movement inside. I waited, knowing that waking them would be rude. Finally, I saw curtains opening and my friend in her pajamas sitting at the table eating cereal. I stepped up the stairs, knocked at the door, and waited. My heart did its own knocking in my chest. Soon after, Cindy came to the door, her dark blonde hair wild and uncombed, green eyes still unwashed, joined by her older sister, a mirror image.

"Hey! Hi! Come in, come in!" Cindy screamed in excitement as she hugged me and led me inside. Their small but comfortable mobile home was perfect; Cindy and her sister, Kathy, fussed over me like a brand-new doll. Their mother and father stood nearby, looking confused.

"Hi, sweetie, where are your parents?" Cindy's mom asked.

"Home, asleep," I answered politely, trying not to get distracted by Cindy, who was standing by my side grinning.

"Do they know you're here?" Cindy's father asked.

"No," I answered, quickly shaking my head.

"Do you know your phone number?" Cindy's mom asked, concerned.

I shook my head.

"Can we go play?" Cindy asked her parents.

They answered carefully, saying of course it was fine if we played for a while. They were both smiling, so it must be okay that I came.

Cindy and Kathy didn't wait another second for their parents to change their minds, jumping up and down in excitement. Cindy grabbed one of my hands, and Kathy the other, and they led me to their shared bedroom. It was decorated in pink and white, with two white dressers, a television, and two medium-sized, decorated white boxes made of wood, which looked like good places to sit.

"Look!" Cindy said as she knelt on the ground and opened the boxes to reveal their contents. They were filled with toys, including Barbie, Cabbage Patch, and Strawberry Shortcake dolls.

"What do you want to play first?" They both looked at me intently, waiting for an answer.

I shrugged. "What do *you* want to play?" I answered, overwhelmed by so many choices. It didn't take long before a decision was made, and soon play was in full swing. We took a break to eat lunch—bologna sandwich, chips, and Oreo cookies with milk. Later, there was a spaghetti dinner with garlic toast. The food was tasty, satisfying, comforting, and I didn't have to use separate plates, forks, or cup. Best of all, it wasn't oatmeal, or peanut butter and jelly sandwiches with raisins and apple juice.

Their parents came in to check on us throughout the day, standing side by side, both with arms crossed, careful to approach with questions as if I was a deer ready to run. Sometimes they lingered awhile, then talked in hush-hush voices in the living room or in their shared bedroom.

At bedtime, Cindy was more than eager to lend me pajamas. After brushing our teeth, the three of us lay on sleeping bags on the floor side by side. I was in the middle, praying that was okay since I didn't want to get them sick. Ms. Ama would never allow that. They hugged and played with me like I wasn't different. Except for their beauty, I was one of them. Finally, our eyelids got heavy and it was cozy under the warm covers. We fought sleep anyway—laughing, giggling, and making plans for our future (the next few days) until all at once, sleep finally won.

I woke up in the morning next to Cindy and Kathy . . . it wasn't just a dream. We started cleaning up to get ready for breakfast.

"Cindy, come here," her mom called out.

"Coming, Mommy!" she answered and rushed to the living room.

A minute later, she came back to the room, eyes watery.

"Your dad is here," she said to me.

Cindy's mother came up behind her. "Your father is here to pick you up." She smiled.

I was heartbroken. I could hear the exchange of deep male voices in the living room, but the words were unclear. I didn't understand.

"Let her get ready," Cindy's mother said softly as she led away my friend who looked just as sad as I did. I put my running-away clothes back on and walked slowly to the living room. My father was there, in my new home's living room. He looked at me with disappointment. I didn't say anything, just stared at the floor. How could this happen? This was not part of the plan. I had never imagined going back and I didn't have a second plan. It only made sense that once I left, there would be no going back.

All at once, everyone was staring at me. Cindy's parents looked alarmed at my reaction and seemed unsure of what to do.

"Are you okay?" Cindy's father asked. His wife stood next to him, looking confused.

I nodded my head, looking down at the floor. My body flushed with heat and tears welled up in my eyes. I held in the tears.

"Thank you for calling and letting her spend the night," my father said quickly, noting the building discomfort. "I'll find out what's going on. I don't know why she did this. Thanks again. Come on," my father said softly, guiding me to the door by the shoulder. I followed his lead.

Ms. Ama was waiting in the car with the little ones. She was wearing sunglasses, but the heat from her glare caused shivers down my back as I sat down.

"So embarrassing," she commented as my father closed his door.

He was quiet. I wondered what was next. *Will he send me back to my mom?*

I would have been ashes within seconds if Ms. Ama had laser vision. The little pretty ones just looked at me like I was a toy they had lost and now found. During the ride, I glanced quickly at Ms. Ama. She was calm, her lips turned up in a slight smirk. She was glad about what I'd done. I'd disappointed my father. She was right, I was bad. Her perfectly done makeup, flowing silk flowered dress, and the sweet perfume on her creamy white skin were such a contrast to my odious looks and ill-fitting clothes. I looked at her prettiness and touched my hair. I really was an oddball. Why in the world would they look for me? I ruined the picture.

"Why did you do this, Eliza?" my father said, breaking his silence.

"I don't understand. I give her clothes, she has her own room. I don't know, honey," Ms. Ama said, turning her gaze outside the window.

I didn't answer. He got quiet. So did she.

I wondered what she was planning for my punishment. The images played in mind—the tiniest hairs on my skin rose, anticipating the familiar sting.

Does he have to go to work today? No, it's Sunday. It will be tomorrow while he's at work. Probably after school, before he gets home.

I sat in the backseat not saying a word, hoping my silence would grant me some mercy. She didn't have to warn me, she had already done so a thousand times in a language foreign to my father or with the icy glare that was just as potent. I was trained, aware of my boundaries, in fear of the stings that zapped my helpless body.

"I wonder if she's sorry . . . No."

Just as quickly I came to my senses. There would be no apologies for grabbing my hair and hitting my head against the toilet because I missed a spot. No taking pity on my hair and letting me use conditioner on my dried out, tightly kinked hair that resembled a wire scrub brush.

How did I get here? This was supposed to be my dream life, but reality was painful. I looked out the window and stared at the leaves on the ground, the tall, awesome trees, and the clouds that played atop them. I was jealous. They were out, and I was trapped.

It wasn't like that the first day. That had been my dream day.

History

I t was solemn the rest of the day at home. I was comforted by watching baby Jay softly sucking his thumb with his big round eyes, straight shiny hair, and soft bubbly cheeks. Father was home, so I survived the rest of the day. He tried to talk to me, but he might as well have been talking to the wall since I was distracted with thoughts about Ms. Ama. He gave up.

That night, I lay in my bed and wished I was still at Cindy's or even better with my mom. I closed my eyes, hoping to sleep, as warm tears trickled down. I pushed my face against the pillow, turning my cries into snorting whimpers. I kept my eyes shut tight.

Think of something good . . . something good . . . to make yourself forget.

Mom. No one could compare to her natural beauty, her bright smile, and her naturally curly hair—big loose curls that bounced at the slightest movement and caressed my face softly when I was in her embrace.

Sundown, she's stretched out on the hammock, slowly rocking and smoking as she stares into open space. Staring and smoking, smoking and staring, deeply sad, but I was clueless as to the reason.

One day I'm going to be a doctor, I thought, so I can help her. I will fix her broken heart, that's what doctors do.

I pictured our last day together.

"You're going to see your father," she said in Tagalog, her voice cracking yet determined.

"Really? When?" My heart raced with joy.

"I'm going to take you the day after tomorrow."

I screamed in joy. It would be the first time in seven years! I don't even remember what he looked like; I was only two the last time I saw him. I was finally going to see my father again. It was a dream come true, a prayer answered. Going to America was a dream for most of the children—and adults—in the Philippines. It was a chance for a good life and endless possibilities.

Mom was smiling, but I could tell she was sad. I didn't understand why, and she wouldn't say.

I'm not sure exactly how my parents met and ended up together, but my father was stationed in the Philippines in service to the Air Force for some time. I've heard my father speak highly of Filipino women. He was attracted to their mixture of beauty, softness, submissiveness, and loyalty. My parents were married and a year later, my brother, Reginald, was born. What was to be a blessing turned into sorrow when he was stillborn. My father wanted a son and was crushed, my mom even more so. Two years later, I was born. Would I exist had my brother lived?

My father, a charming, black southern gentleman, was five feet ten and about 250 pounds, with a bright white smile. A fine conversationalist, he was outgoing and flirty with the ladies. He was raised in a religious Baptist family and my grandfather was a full-time church pastor while Grandma served as the First Lady. Grandma was sixteen when she met and married my grandpa; he was thirty-three. She worked as an elementary school teacher and took care of the family after work. Uncle David was only eighteen months younger than my father, and they were close throughout their lifetime. They had an older brother who ran away from home before they were even born. It was a family secret no one liked to talk about. He never came back. I wondered why and asked my Uncle David, but he didn't know. I didn't have the courage to ask Grandma, it might hurt her too much. My father went to college but didn't graduate. He enlisted in the Air Force during the draft for the Vietnam War. Uncle David enlisted in the Army.

Mom was a naturally beautiful, petite (4'11") Filipina, who believed in hard work. She didn't like owing anyone anything and was not afraid to get her hands dirty—working on cars, motorcycles, and whatever needed to get fixed. She had a tomboy streak, stubborn, independent, and generous—she would help anyone if she could. The only exception to the rule was her mother. From what I was told, Mom and her brother were sent away by their mother to be raised by their grandparents but brought up the rest of her children. This left the two children feeling abandoned. She never shared her story with my brother or me, but her feelings and intentions were clear and obvious.

From the bits of history I learned from my father, he and my mother were incompatible. She was outspoken, enjoying social gatherings and her independence. My father preferred a soft-spoken homemaker. He said they often argued, which he disliked, as he naturally shies away from conflict. I don't remember ever hearing them fight, but I don't remember living with them together for too long, either.

According to Aunt Letty, I was about two years old when my parents divorced. Mom had no idea that she was signing divorce papers—she believed she was signing papers to buy furniture. Her English and education were quite limited. She remained a Filipino citizen and had no money or resources to fight my father for custody. I was a California-born American citizen and gaining full custody of me was a given for my father, leaving Mom with no right to me. According to the system, she no longer had a daughter.

Following legal finalizations, my father was ordered back to the United States. Our future had been decided, in part by strangers. Mom was stripped of her marriage, which caused her shame since she was Catholic. She was replaced by another woman and now, losing her daughter all at once was crushing her world and heart.

Aunt Letty told this story to Ronnie and me like a legend. She was dramatic, but at least it gave me some reasons for my mom's pain.

My New Family

I had first joined my father's family about a year or so before that Saturday I ran away. It didn't bother me when my father didn't let me take any of my things with me to America. He said something as I gathered them, and my mom nodded and explained it to me. This way I would have new clothes and I could use the old dresses when I visited her.

My father said something I didn't understand.

Mom took me aside. "Be a good girl and listen to your father and his wife. You're going to live with them, your sister, and brother, but I'm going to see you soon. *Mahal Kita* (I love you)," she said, hugging me. I wasn't worried. We had done this so many times before and we always came back together.

"*Mahal Kita po*," I responded. I saw the tears she held back in the shallows of her eyes, but I didn't understand. If only I had.

Taking my hand, my father led me away. I looked back at my mother—her eyes were teary and her body rigid. Maybe she needed another hug.

No matter, I'll see her again soon.

My father and I walked toward the army base, where a woman and two children stood. This was my new family—my father's wife, my brother, and my sister. They were all stunning and they smelled nice too! Soon, I would smell like them; right now, I didn't smell so good.

My father said some things in English, but all I understood were their names—Ama, Candace, Jason.

"It's nice to meet you, Eliza," Ms. Ama said in Tagalog as she extended her hand.

Ms. Ama was strikingly attractive—Chinese-Filipina, with creamy white skin, perfectly applied makeup, mid-length stylish light brown straight hair, wearing a silky multicolored dress and black low-pumped heels. She was so different from Mom. I have never seen my mom wear makeup or jewelry or a dress, let alone a fancy one.

I decided to call her Ms. Ama, but possibly "Ate," which means "elder sister," as a sign of respect.

She held a handsome, smiling boy of about two years, Jason, wearing a blue and white shorts outfit and shiny black shoes. Standing close to her was the cutest four-year-old girl wearing a yellow dress and black shoes. She had long dark hair and light caramel-colored skin, and was holding a black doll with short curled hair, dressed in yellow pajamas. The doll made a bell sound when shaken, but her eyes stayed open without blinking and its face had a stationary smile.

"This is for you." Candace stretched out her hand to gift me the doll.

"Thank you," I said, smiling from ear to ear. In my sporadic school days, I managed to learn a few polite American phrases like "Hello," "Good-bye," and "Thank you." The Filipino teachers tried to prepare us for days such as this, just in case one or two of us were lucky enough. I was looking forward to learning more.

My father said some things I didn't understand and kissed me on the forehead. Ms. Ama kindly translated for me. I nodded with a huge smile.

My father left and the four of us headed toward a car.

"Get in," Ms. Ama said kindly in Tagalog.

My eyes widened. *I get to ride in a car. They have a car—they're rich!*

Ms. Ama put Jason in a special seat I had never seen before in the middle backseat of the car. I sat next to him and Candace climbed in the front passenger side. Jason was looking at me, smiling from ear to ear like I was a new toy. *What a sweet little boy,* I thought.

We went to a department store where Ms. Ama bought me new clothes, including socks and underwear, plus a pair of shoes. Everything I needed. I had fantasized about this so many times but couldn't believe it was happening. Soon after, Jason got cranky and needed a nap, stopping short the shopping spree.

Ms. Ama drove home to drop Jason off with the nanny so he could take a comfortable nap. He fell asleep after crying hard in the car. I waited for directions, thinking we would go inside the house. Ms. Ama had a different plan.

"We're going out to lunch and then to a hair salon," she said, "so they can fix your hair."

Really? My heart jumped with joy. *Someone pinch me, I'm dreaming!*

We went to a restaurant for lunch, which was also a first-time experience. I can't remember what I ate, probably because I ate it too fast, but it was delicious. Ms. Ama just watched me, seeming delighted, and encouraged me to eat. Afterward, we went to the beauty salon where a black lady with a long curly hairstyle, wearing a black floral dress under an apron, approached us. She looked at me, smiled, touched my hair, curious, and turned to Ms. Ama and said some things I didn't understand. Ms. Ama responded, shrugged, and shook her head. The stylist looked at me again, smiled, and directed me to her chair. *What were they saying?*

When we left the salon, I had a totally different look—tiny braids that began in "corn rows" on my head, with colorful decorative beads at their ends. Later, Ms. Ama shared that the stylist said I had "bad hair" because it was hard and dry, so they chose this hairstyle. I quietly agreed. My hair had always been a lot of trouble for me; it grew out like dry grass. With my new hairstyle, every time I moved my head the beads hit each other noisily like a set of bells ringing on my head, or if I moved too fast sideways, they hit my face. I tried not to move. I wished I had my mother's bouncy, loosely curled hair or Ms. Ama's straight, shiny, sweet-smelling hair that rested on her shoulders.

"Maybe we'll just cut it all off one day and start over," Ms. Ama suggested, smiling, when we left the salon.

We ended up at an ice cream shop for dessert. Picking a flavor from so many choices was overwhelming, but I settled on rocky road with chunks of marshmallows and almonds brimming over the side of the cone.

When we arrived home, I couldn't wait to see what the inside looked like. Right inside the front door was the entryway leading to a hallway toward the bedrooms, and to the right was the living room, nicely furnished with a sofa, love seat, recliner, and coffee and end tables. The large wall-to-wall entertainment center was filled with electronics—television, stereo, a videocassette player, and lots and lots of movies. Next to it was the dining room with a grand shiny table long enough to seat eight people, a china cabinet with fancy dishes, and a large painting of the Last Supper hanging on the wall as a reminder of Christ's love and sacrifice for humanity. To the left of the dining area was a kitchen, with a small table and four chairs. A maid was busy cooking dinner. She stopped just long enough to greet us and then went back to work. In the few minutes I was in the kitchen, she opened cupboards, the refrigerator, and the pantry to find various ingredients for the meal. I couldn't believe how much food there was to eat. Everywhere I looked, there was food!

I was led to a room across from the kitchen.

"This is your room," Ms. Ama said, standing by the doorway as she motioned me in, Candace standing close to her as I walked in.

"Can't she sleep with me in my room?" Candace asked longingly.

"No," Ms. Ama quickly answered. Candace pouted.

I looked into the room with two twin beds nicely covered with floral decorated quilts. A nightstand separated the beds and a lamp was on top of it.

"The maids use this room, too, but that's your bed over there." She pointed to the far side of the room.

"There's the closet for your clothes and this is your dresser." She stood next to a four-drawer dresser with a laundry basket full of clothes waiting for the maid to sort it out.

"*Maraming salamat po,*" I said, which means "thank you, respectfully."

"Go ahead and put your clothes away," Ms. Ama directed. "The bathroom is down here when you need to use it."

"*Maraming salamat po,*" I repeated. Ms. Ama walked away and entered one of the rooms down the hall with Candace in tow.

I looked around my room. "I have my own clean bed!" I exclaimed.

I laid my new baby doll on my pillow and set the bags of clothes on my bed to sort through them. I admired and appreciated each item out of the bag, smoothing each one as I put them in drawers or hung them in the closet. I was so lucky.

I took a few steps down the hallway—I had to look at the bathroom. I flicked the switch and straight across was a tub, covered by a curtain. Just a step ahead to my left was the sink with soap in a colorful container. So pretty! I turned the sink knob and *voila*, running water. Fascinating!

Ouch! That one was hot, the other was for cold.

A few steps further was a shiny white toilet. I looked in—clean water, nothing else as far in as I could see, and it didn't smell. I pushed down the silver toggle...it flushed! "Whoa!" I whispered as I watched the water swirl down. *Amazing!*

I pushed the tub curtains aside to see what was in there. Shampoo, soap, conditioner, but what was the metal thing coming from the wall?

"That's a shower," Ms. Ama told me, standing by the doorway, Candace right next to her with red eyes. She was still upset.

"Water comes from there while you wash yourself. You just turn these." She pointed to two knobs. "You should take a shower before dinner. There's soap and here is a shower cap so your hair won't get wet."

"*Maraming salamat, po.*" I nodded thankfully.

Ms. Ama turned on the shower, showing me how to balance between the two knobs for the best temperature and a comfortable shower. Once confident I understood, she left me alone with a towel and washcloth.

I grabbed some clothes and went back into the bathroom to do this "shower." I turned the knobs, balanced the water, and then pulled another silver knob, just as Ms. Ama said. Water came out fast and full force, startling me a little. I stuck my hand out to see how it would feel, and that didn't help. I put on what she called a shower cap, another weird thing, and braved it in the tub.

It was my own rainfall, but it was so fast, slightly stinging my flesh. My first position wasn't good, so water splashed all over my face, scaring me a bit. I backed up. After a minute or so, I finally relaxed. It was nice and odd at the same time, but afterward, I was so clean! I dried myself, put some lotion on like Ms. Ama said, hung the shower cap up to dry, and put on some new clothes. I took a deep breath. I smelled nice.

That night, Ms. Ama's father and sister came over to visit and welcomed me to the family. Ms. Ama and her father looked so much alike and I could tell he was an important man. He was very friendly. Her sister was just as attractive, dressed just as nice, and smelled just as incredible. Ms. Ama and her family were what we considered rich Filipinos with nice comfortable homes (flushable toilets included), plenty of food, a car, and comfort.

There was a feast of food, both Filipino and American cuisine, in my honor. My father had an event to attend for work, so Ms. Ama told me he would see me later before I went to sleep. Jason sat in his high chair next to Ms. Ama with a plate of food, refusing to eat. Candace sat on the other side of Ms. Ama staring at me with a smile, while her mother prompted her to eat. The little girl was clearly distracted with all that was happening. I had no problem eating and talked in between swallows as they laughed and listened. I made sure to say my grace of thanks to God—I was definitely grateful.

"Oh, that's good. You have good manners," they said, impressed. I smiled. My mom raised me well.

Ms. Ama's sister and father asked one question after another in Tagalog, interested in all my experiences.

"Where did you live?"

"We didn't have a house, so we stayed with family or friends. We were in Dau with my grandma for a while; my brother is still there, I'm going to visit them soon," I said. They looked at me with pity and responded with "Ohhh."

"Did you go to school?"

"No, my mom didn't have money." More sounds and looks of pity.

In between my responses, I ate. I ate so much, my stomach hurt, but it was all so tasty delicious. Everyone just laughed at or pitied whatever I said. Occasionally I looked to see Ms. Ama's reaction to all that was going on. She just looked at me intently, and occasionally, she would say something to her family in Kapampangan—a dialect I didn't understand. But mostly she listened quietly as the other two chimed in with all their questions.

After dinner, there was dessert of all types. I had never seen so much food in my life and I ate as much as my little bony body could hold. Finally, it was time for the small people to go to bed, which included me, and two maids busied themselves with the cleanup. I offered to help, but Ms. Ama said, "No, you don't need to help, they will take care of it. You get ready for bed. Brush your teeth."

I nodded and obeyed. I brushed my teeth, changed into pajamas, lay down, and pulled my covers over me. Ahhh, so nice! My body tingled, sending me into a fit of giggles. I grabbed my doll and hugged it tight. I was sleepy from everything that had happened. But just as I was about to fall asleep, there was a soft knock at my door. My father peeked in and said something I still didn't understand. I sat up, smiling with welcome.

He walked in, followed by Ms. Ama and Candace.

He came over to my bedside, said more things I didn't understand, and then said, "Good night," which I understood. He kissed me on the forehead and turned around to rejoin his wife and daughter to leave. "Good night," Candace said. "Good night," Ms. Ama repeated and closed the door behind them. What a nice family.

I closed my eyes and relived everything that had happened in my mind. What could possibly happen next? I lay back down to ready for sleep. I prayed, saying some prayers for my mom and Ronnie. I wished I could share all of this with them. Ronnie would be so ecstatic. Maybe next time they would let him come, too. I thought I would ask Ms. Ama if I could bring them something, maybe some food. *They would like that.* I fell asleep fantasizing about what it would be like to have Ronnie and Mom here with me in Wonderland and imagined them enjoying the food I was planning to bring.

I woke up bright and early the next day, glad it wasn't just a dream. I got up right away, as I didn't want to seem lazy. I changed out of my pajamas and into one of my new outfits. The smell of my new clothes was intoxicating.

"*Magandang umaga (Good morning)*," Ms. Ama said, as I opened the door to go to the bathroom. She was already sitting at the kitchen table drinking coffee.

"*Magandang umaga po*," I answered respectfully.

"She's making breakfast now, so finish getting dressed and you can eat," she said in Tagalog.

"*Opo (Yes, respectfully)*." I nodded. I looked into the kitchen and saw Jason sitting in his high chair complaining about having to eat and Candace sitting at the table eating something I had never seen before. The aroma was appetizing, and I wondered what it was.

In the bathroom, I brushed my teeth and washed my face; since my hair was in braids, I didn't have to wrestle with it. I went in the kitchen to eat the food I had never seen before.

"That's pancakes and that's waffles," Candace said, noticing my confusion. I smiled hungrily.

Along with it, they brought out bacon, sausages, orange juice, and milk.

Ms. Ama prepared a plate and took it to my father, who was reading a newspaper in the formal dining room.

"Hi, baby," he called out to me.

I smiled. "Hello," I responded.

I sat down at the dining room table, and the maid prepared my plate.

Candace was delighted to tell me the next steps to this new cuisine, which was to cut up the flat circle-shaped, aroma filled bread-like food, pour sticky brown fluid on it, and eat it. I followed her instructions and it was delicious. Candace enjoyed watching me eat more than she liked eating her own breakfast, but the maid praised her for finally eating all her food. Apparently, this wasn't a normal thing and watching me encouraged her. Imagine that. They had all this food, but didn't like to eat. Where I came from, we didn't have much, but we ate everything, nothing was ever wasted.

For the next two months life was wonderful. Candace and Jason had so many toys in the room they shared that there was barely enough space to move around. Candace must have had every girl toy from Barbie dolls, regular dolls, and baby dolls, little houses, cars, mini stoves, mini refrigerator, mini dishes and cups. We played to our hearts' content. She was glad to have a playmate, but at the same time, she was used to doing as she pleased, so she was always directing our play. Jason was no different. He was as mischievous as he was cute, and it was difficult for the nanny to control either of them. Occasionally, Jason played with us, but after a few minutes, would get bored and do something else. I adored them both, even with their bossy stubbornness. I was fitting right in, feeling like a part of the family.

What Just Happened?

Every afternoon, Candace, Jason, and I went outside to play while Ms. Ama planned dinner with the maid. Candace and Jason played with other kids their age until we were called in for dinner. As the oldest, I was left in charge of the young ones, so I didn't get to play, just watched them.

One day, Jason was especially mischievous, picking up rocks and throwing them anywhere and everywhere.

"Stop it. No!" I repeated several times, growing afraid he would hit someone.

Jason just looked at me with a smirk on his face and kept throwing rocks. My commands had no effect. Candace was busy playing with another little girl her age with dolls and cars.

"Stop! No," I warned him, still limited in my vocabulary.

Suddenly, the cute face had a wide grin on it and before I knew it, a rock the size of a large grape was coming fast toward me. I had no chance to move. *Smack!* The rock hit the center of my forehead, breaking the skin. Warm blood trickled down and in seconds the spot had formed into a sizable knot. I was in shock and so was everyone else—jaws dropped in disbelief. Jason stood there, with a grin still on his face, and began giggling. When I finally snapped out of my stupor, I realized Jason had a larger rock in his hand ready to aim and fire again. I rushed over to him, afraid I would get hit again or worse, someone else would. I dislodged his grip from the rock and with his palm exposed, I slapped it once with my fingers and told him "No!" He stopped, looked at me, and began to cry loudly.

"Mommy . . . Mommy!!" he wailed. The hit was barely hard enough to swat a fly. The nannies had trouble controlling him, and I had wondered why they never disciplined him. He would hit the maids, run away, and ignore them, all the while laughing as he terrorized. I didn't understand it. Where I came from, respect toward our elders was expected from all children, as was obedience, which we learned from an early age.

Ms. Ama heard Jason's cries and came outside to comfort him. She called Candace over to find out what happened while I stood in shock a few feet away. Ms. Ama glared at me, focused in on my forehead, and stood up. Within a minute, satisfied that he'd made trouble, Jason stopped his dry cry and bounced back to play, picking rocks up again. Ms. Ama grabbed my left ear with her right thumb and forefinger, dug her nails in, and twisted, leading me by the ear into the house.

"You don't hit my kids!" she hissed, shoving me into my room and closing the door behind me.

I sat on my bed and waited. *What's going on? What's happening?*

A minute later, she returned, darkening my doorway with a big black belt coiled around her right hand. Her face was no longer recognizable. The beauty was gone—one eyebrow spiked high, lips and eyes tightened, and creamy white skin now flushed with anger. The words that spewed from her mouth were loud, but I didn't hear anything—shock had taken over. She entered my room and closed the door.

The beating lasted minutes, but to me it was forever. When she finally left, my mind was blank. Tears streamed down my face. My body was broken in so many ways, inside and out.

"Don't you ever touch my children again!"

I sat on my bed. I couldn't stand up, my body involuntarily quaking. Blood stained my disarrayed sheets while I held tight to my pillow for comfort. My bottom lip and ears were bleeding from her nails and my arms and legs ached. I touched a large scratch on the side of my face.

"Clean all that up and go back outside and watch them," she ordered as she walked to the kitchen.

"Back outside?" I tried to stand up, but my knees buckled in weakness. I sat back down on my bed to catch myself. *Oh God! I better hurry.*

I got up shakily, straightened up my bed, changed my bloodied clothes, and wiped my face as best as I could before I walked outside. The other children stared at me in silence. I saw pity and disbelief, like they were watching a train crash. What had just happened? I couldn't say anything. Deeply embarrassed, I stood far off, wishing they would stop staring.

Candace was playing dolls with her friend and Jason had moved on to finding bugs. I stood in a daze. I looked at my arms, then my legs—*what were these colors, these blotches of red and blue?* After touching them, my finger ricocheted back up. My whole body hurt. I touched the back of my throbbing ear and when I looked at my fingers, they were covered in blood and pieces of my skin. I didn't get to wipe back there. I whimpered. *I can't cry out here. What does this mean? Will my father save me? Oh God, help me!*

When my father came home, Candace couldn't wait to tell him all about the most exciting event of the day. He sat at the formal dining room table waiting for his plate of food, which was being prepared by his wife. He sat Candace on his lap, listening to her intently, very much a loving father. He grimaced at first, but then his face relaxed. Jason came over to join them—after all, this was his story—and his father kissed him lovingly. Dinner was served. They sat as a family together at the table. I stayed in the kitchen.

They were a sight of love. Mother and father, both tender with their children. Blessed.

Later, at bedtime, my father came and sat by my bedside. Ms. Ama was standing at the doorway. Her expression was cold and stern, but only I could see that, since my father's back faced her.

He asked questions, touching the knot on my forehead. I was silent.

He kept talking, his tone concerned as he touched the side of my face. The scratch was no longer numb. I got a flash of how I got it. I looked at Ms. Ama.

He kissed my forehead, told me goodnight, got up, and left, closing the door behind him.

Once alone, my body shook again. I touched the side of my face where my father's fingers had showed he cared. My body drained by pain, I didn't have enough courage to look at the bruises under my clothes. A flood of tears flowed uncontrollably—I sank my face in my pillow to muffle my sobs.

I cried out for my mom, my voice cracking in despair.

It's best that Mom is not here. She would be disappointed that I made Ms. Ama mad and got in trouble. I need to be better, I can't let Mom down.

My heart ached. I missed her. I missed Ronnie. My mind escaped to join them. Ronnie and I were outside playing; Mom was watching us, sitting nearby smoking a cigarette and talking to a friend. I looked over and she smiled, her eyes filled with love for us. I cried until I had no strength left. Thankfully, sleep saved me.

The Morning After

My world had shifted. There was no doubt that things had changed. The maids looked at me with sadness and pity. What did Ms. Ama tell them? Ms. Ama glared at me, all softness gone, setting a fire of fear in my heart and body. I wished I hadn't hit Jason, maybe then she would still like me.

"Come play with me," Candace said.

I shook my head. I had no interest in playing or doing anything. I was confused, disappointed, scared.

Candace left, pouting and disappointed. A minute later, she returned. "My mom said you *have* to play with me," she said, her tone dripping with superiority.

Ms. Ama stood down the hall. "Play with her," she demanded coldly, sending chills through my already tense body. I obeyed.

On Saturday mornings, Candace and Jason loved to watch Bugs Bunny, Looney Toons, Mickey and Minnie Mouse, and Donald Duck, just to name a few. They had videocassettes of their favorite cartoon characters and movies, and watched them religiously on weekends.

After breakfast, the routine was to go in the living room in pajamas, agree and/or fight about which movie to watch, and put the videocassette in the player. Then the excitement began. They laughed as though it was their first time seeing the show, although it was clearly not, since they recited the words from memory. I was right there with them, Candace insisting I sit next to her.

After breakfast, I put my dishes in the sink and started clearing the table, which still had Candace's and Jason's plates and spilled food on the floor. "No, go watch cartoons, go on!" Ms. Betty, the maid, demanded to me, smiling as she motioned me out. "I don't need your help. Go on!"

I didn't like leaving her with a mess, but I obeyed. I went to the living room to join Candace and Jason and sat down on the floor. Onscreen, the Tasmanian Devil was on the move. I grinned. It reminded me of Jason with all that energy. They were both adorable but mischievous. Not long after, Ms. Ama stood at the side of the television and looked at me.

"Go help clean up in the kitchen," she said coldly. I jumped up quickly and headed to the kitchen.

"But I want her to watch it with me," Candace objected in a whine.

"No, she can't," Ms. Ama quickly responded. Candace didn't fight the new rule, sensing her mother's tone, and redirected her focus to the television. Giggles followed. I joined Ms. Betty in the kitchen and hoped she wasn't disappointed that I was in there getting in her way. I smiled sheepishly, hoping for a welcome, like a stray dog looking for a treat. She looked at me; sadness filled her eyes and she drew me close for a quick hug while she shook her head. Just as quickly, she backed away in case Ms. Ama decided to come and check on me. Quietly, I let out a sigh of relief since Ms. Betty was okay with me. We both went back to work. I cleared the table, she washed the dishes. I belonged in the kitchen with her, doing exactly what I was doing. I was safe.

Since then, every Saturday, I would get up early in the morning and clean with Ms. Betty. Occasionally, after all the cleaning was done, I stood by the wall at the end of the hallway which separated the living room from the dining room to catch a glimpse of the onscreen fun. But somehow, since things had changed, I began to see the characters differently. They became my teachers in survival. Like Bugs Bunny, who was funny, smart, and elusive. He would find himself in trouble, sometimes even in dangerous situations, but he always used his intelligence and creativity to get out of it. Others, like the Road Runner, simply ran very fast. They were all my heroes.

When I didn't have enough courage to take the chance of getting caught, I just stayed in my room and looked at unwanted books. I looked at the pictures and made up the words to match them. I couldn't go to school because I needed shots. I had to start from the beginning like a newborn baby, especially since I was coming from a "third world country." They weren't taking chances in case I had a disease. Following months of my living with them, Ms. Ama decided that I should have my own separate cup, bowl, plate, fork, and spoon to use for my meals. I couldn't use any others' dishes or cutlery, and no one could use mine. I had my own soap and shampoo, and my own set of towels.

"Honey, I don't want anyone else to get sick," she explained to my father. He didn't resist—he let it go. Did she do the same when she prepared to go to America? Did she separate herself, too? What about the baby in her tummy? The maids were even more confused since they were native Filipinas and had never had shots; they didn't have to use separate utensils and they cooked our daily meals. I hoped that in the last three months of using the same things, I hadn't infected them; so far nothing had come up.

When I finally had enough shots so I could go to school, I was thrilled. By now, I was ten years old and a blank slate, but they couldn't put me in kindergarten because I was too old, and they couldn't put me in sixth grade because of my academic skill level. They decided to put me in a younger class, but one that was nearest my age group—fifth grade. I didn't understand much of what was going on in class. Back then, there were no ESL classes, and no one understood me, so I relied heavily on body language.

My teacher, Ms. Babbitt, was tasked with the challenge of helping me catch up.

On my first day, I was amazed at the classroom—a wonderland decorated with numbers, alphabets, and colors, with stacks of shiny books in big cabinets. The other students were like Candace and Jason, content and privileged with no worries in the world. They must have had parents like my father and Ms. Ama. I had been like that, underprivileged, but content and safe, when I lived with my mom.

"Good morning, class," Ms. Babbitt said, smiling, her hand on my shoulder. "We have a new student, Eliza Jackson. I want you to make her feel welcome." It was awkward standing in front of everyone, especially the way I looked. These people were all so pretty, including my blonde-haired, blue-eyed teacher. Before going to school, I hadn't seen people with blond or light hair or light-colored eyes, but apparently there were many of them. How did they get to be so perfect?

Ms. Babbitt's touch on my shoulder gave me comfort. I was safe. The students respected her and I didn't see anyone giving me a weird look.

"Sit over there, next to Cindy," she directed. A girl raised her hand high with a big grin to help me find my way. Despite our language barrier, Cindy and I became instant friends. I admired her long, wavy blonde hair and sparkling eyes. I expected she would treat me differently, but instead, she was pleasant and curious.

School became my home—my safe place and my retreat. There, I could be myself and forget about where I lived. I didn't want to miss a moment, and I dreaded days when we didn't go to school, like weekends. Why couldn't we go to school every day? I couldn't wait until the sun came up, brightening up my room and waking me up to get dressed. I barely understood basic English and even less math. At home, I spoke to Ms. Ama and Ms. Betty mostly in Tagalog, but in time, I learned more through repetition. I only had a few months of education in a Filipino elementary public school since Mom couldn't afford it and we were constantly moving. My situation was common there; everything in the Philippines costs money, including education.

My ignorance was no match for my love and commitment to learn—I dove in headfirst, embracing every opportunity that was given to me. Ms. Babbitt encouraged me with patience. I began to understand more and more as she taught, and I watched others respond.

"Good morning, class!" Ms. Babbitt would say every morning. It was the best sound. I loved to hear it each morning, no matter how many times I had already heard it.

"Good morning, Ms. Babbitt!" we all responded. I truly meant it.

"Let's stand for the Pledge of Allegiance. Put your right hand over your heart," she continued as the announcement was heard over the classroom loudspeaker. It reminded me of when I used to recite similar words in a Filipino school, except we all stood on the front school lawn, all together in unison. This allegiance thing must mean a lot to people no matter where you go.

During lunch, Cindy and I sat together. She had an older sister named Kathy, but she sat with her friends at a different table. After a few weeks of sitting together, Cindy asked, "Why do you eat the same thing every day?"

I was quiet. *How can I answer?*

It was true, every day Ms. Ama had the maid make me a peanut butter and jelly sandwich, apple juice, and raisins. Candace had a variety of her choosing—things like bologna or turkey sandwiches, fruit snacks, Jell-O cups, crackers, cookies, chips, and fruits, whatever she desired. I couldn't give an explanation and Cindy realized it and saw that the question brought me sadness.

"It's okay. You want some of mine?" she asked.

That was the first and last time she asked about my lunch, but she would always offer me items from her lunch box. Some days, she would practically force me to accept because I readily refused, thanking her in the process, but shaking my head vigorously.

At the end of each day, when the bell rang, my heart sank. It was worst on Fridays. One day, before I could leave the classroom, Ms. Babbitt stopped me.

"Eliza, wait a minute."

I stopped. *Did I do something bad? I hope I'm not in trouble.*

"Here are some books I think you will like. The more you read, the faster you will learn," she said, handing me two books.

"Thank you," I said, and smiled at her, grateful for the kindness. *I'm no one special, why would she do that for me?*

"You can return these books whenever you finish, and you may borrow another when you're ready," she added.

"Thank you," I repeated in gratitude.

She smiled, lifting my gloomy spirit.

I couldn't wait for the chance to read the books. I went over my "once I get home" to-do list in my head: do my homework, watch the kids outside, eat, and help clean up from dinner.

Finally, when all the to-dos were over and I was alone in my room for bedtime, I lay in my bed and opened one of the books. It was a simple mystery book in basic, first grade language, but it triggered my imagination. While I was reading, nothing else existed—not in that world, not in mine.

I was deep in the story, solving the mystery, all the while wondering what's going to happen next? What magic is this? I read nonstop until I finished both books. Disappointed that my adventure was over, I stayed in the fantasy world until I fell asleep.

The following day, I returned both books to Ms. Babbitt.

"You finished them?" she asked.

"Yes, ma'am," I answered. Ms. Babbitt smiled.

"Would you like to borrow more?" she asked. I nodded.

"Good, whenever you're ready you can go over to the cabinet and pick out whatever you want to read, and just return them when you're done." Ms. Babbitt pointed at the cabinets filled with books. "You can also write a book report about each one for extra credit."

"Thank you," I responded, nearly overcome with gratitude.

"You're welcome," was always her answer.

Since that day, all my free time was spent at my new favorite spot, the cabinet, to find my new adventures. Each weekday night, I brought two books home. I took three or four home during the weekends, and anticipated the time when I could be alone. Alone time was a great time.

I needed to read as much as I needed to breathe. I wished I could be in school all the time, but the books gave me an escape while I was home. I read constantly, even through the night, using a flashlight. I finished at least one to two books a night, wrote a report about each of them, and turned them in daily. Ms. Babbitt was surprised, but was delighted at my commitment, even writing it on my progress reports: "She is a pleasure to have in class, eager to learn." The more I read, the more I learned and advanced. The people who wrote those books helped me escape my life and gave me reason to hope. *Could Ms. Ama take this from me?*

This Is Home

"Jason, eat your food! You're gonna be hungry later on," Ms. Ama bellowed.

"I don't want it, I'm full," Jason whined as he made faces, sinking lower and lower in his seat until all we could see was his tiny little head above the table.

"I'm full too, Mom, you gave me too much," Candace joined in. "Can I watch TV now?" she asked.

"Give your food to Eliza, she'll eat it," Ms. Ama said, peering at me through the corner of her eye as she sipped her coffee.

I looked up, confused. I still had mounds of food to finish myself.

Jason and Candace were ecstatic and didn't waste a minute, plopping their leftover food on top of mine.

What in the world?

Ms. Betty just looked at me, up then down, without a word. Was Ms. Ama trying to get me fat? Usually, the leftover food went in the garbage disposal. I ate and ate in silent obedience. The food pushed through every curve and corner of my stomach until there was no more room to give. I writhed in pain, eyes welling up with tears, my breathing short and shallow. I held it in, afraid to make things worse.

"Hurry up!" Ms. Ama ordered. Candace and Jason were already watching their favorite shows, their laughter echoing throughout the house. I had promised Mom I would be good. I swallowed another bite.

Afterward, I cleaned with Ms. Betty and cared for the little ones, a little stooped from pain, but Ms. Betty understood.

On the weekends, Ms. Betty and the maids were off, so I got up early in the morning to dust, sweep, and mop the house, and scrub the bathrooms. While Ms. Ama was pregnant, Ms. Betty worked on Saturdays to help. Now, Ms. Ama started giving Ms. Betty the weekends off again. Ms. Betty told me Ms. Ama was an excellent maid before she married my father, so she had high expectations. I was young, but I had to learn quickly. Most days I hoped I did well. Most of the time, I was on my knees to make sure everything was clean, especially the bottom parts of the toilet.

"Where's the Clorox?" Ms. Ama asked. I opened the cabinet under the sink and moved the Ajax, which was blocking the view. Ajax and Clorox were my cleaning buddies. According to Ms. Ama, it was not clean if they were not used. In fact, they were cleaning me, too; the reek of Clorox didn't go away for at least a day. I leaned back and pointed so she could see it.

"Okay, make sure you use them and scrub hard," she ordered, slipping on a pair of gloves to clean in the kitchen. "I don't want to see any dirt when you're done, you hear me!"

I looked at my hands, which were scaled, dry, and raw. I wished I had a pair of gloves, and something for my knees too—the constant kneeling to clean and scrub had taken its toll. At least everything would be clean for when Ms. Betty came back to work on Monday. I smiled. By the time I was done, everything was shiny, no spots, and the smell of Clorox was overpowering.

Since my hair had been braided for some time, it was beginning to become more manageable with the help of shampoo and conditioner.

"We need to cut your hair," Ms. Ama said one day after my hair had been unbraided and brushed out.

I looked at her, confused.

"Your grandmother won't recognize you with long hair, so we should cut it so she will know you," she continued with a slight smile.

"Okay," I replied eagerly, glad to be singled out for any attention.

"We can do it in the bathroom. Get a chair from the kitchen, we can do it now," she added.

No beauty shop like before? No going to get my hair cut like everyone else?

Ms. Ama went into her room and joined me in the bathroom holding a pair of scissors. I was already sitting on the chair. I looked up, she gave me another smile, and I returned the expression in kind. She busied herself making quick, rhythmless clipping sounds with the scissors. I was sitting too low to see the mirror, but I could see my hair falling liberally on the ground, clump by clump, until all at once the room was quiet.

"You can get up now," she said and backed away, looking at the mirror, satisfied.

I stood up and looked at my hair—odd-shaped and uneven, resembling an octagon. I was ashamed. I looked harder. *Maybe if I comb it a certain way . . .* My heart began to thump in my chest as tears formed in my eyes. I touched my head; there were empty spaces. I was ugly. I didn't look at Ms. Ama directly. She might get mad.

What do I say?

"Hurry up and clean all this up before it goes in the hallway," she ordered.

I went to the kitchen, grabbed the broom and dust pan, and returned to pick up my locks to be thrown in the trash. Ms. Ama went to her room, which gave me time to whimper. I touched a few strands, but I couldn't take the chance of being seen in case she came back out. Tears quietly rolled down my cheeks as I mourned my lost hair, but sound was not an option. I heard footsteps coming and wiped the tears unnoticed.

"Here!" Ms. Ama said, handing me a bar of Ivory soap. "When you're done, take a shower and wash your hair. Don't get hair all over the place," she said sternly.

I looked at the soap and asked, "What about for my hair?"

"Use the soap! Hurry up!" she answered, clearly annoyed by my question.

I finished cleaning and showered. I washed my hair with the bar of soap, feeling it stiffen even as it was pressed with moisture. Ms. Ama required that I shower and wash my hair every day, so, as days passed, my hair became dry, coarse, and hard. Soon it matched my hands and knees. I had a feeling using soap would make it worse. I dreaded combing it because of the pain and what sounded like electricity as the comb tried to make its way out.

"What happened to your hair?" my father asked a few days after the haircut.

"I cut it, honey," Ms. Ama intervened quickly.

I looked at the ground, waiting to be dismissed. This conversation would for sure make me cry.

"Why did you cut it?" he asked, a hint of annoyance in his voice.

"That way your mom will recognize her, honey," she answered.

He frowned. "You didn't need to cut it all off," he replied, getting a closer look at my uneven hair. "Don't worry, baby, it will grow back," he said to me.

I nodded my head and went to my room, hoping that was the end of it. Ms. Ama stood watching me go. They talked some more going into their room, but I didn't listen. I hoped my father would drop the subject, otherwise Ms. Ama was going to be upset and I would be the one to pay.

During my two years with my new family, Ms. Ama gave birth to my half-brother Jay and soon after, Casey. They were just as lovely as Jason and Candace—making their parents even prouder. I ruined their perfect picture with my coarse afro hair and darker skin. Ms. Ama's disgusted voice saying "You're ugly" rang continuously in my head as she looked at me with contempt. I was ashamed. Why did I have to be here? I was letting my mother down and was an ongoing disappointment to my father.

Ms. Ama had a seamstress who came to the home once a month to make everyone clothes, including a few for me. I had about seven sets of clothes which I rotated wearing for school each day. My brothers' and sister's closets, however, could barely close because they had so many. When it was time to take the yearly family photo, she had the seamstress make matching orange outfits for everyone, all except me. Mine was checkered pink.

"We didn't have enough material," Ms. Ama explained to my father as the family dressed for the yearly photo.

"How did that happen, you couldn't get more?" my father answered, upset.

"No, it was too late," Ms. Ama abruptly answered, making no mention that the outfits had been hanging in the closets for at least two months to make sure they fit each child perfectly. The seamstress was still at the house during their conversation and looked as though she had something to say, but she didn't. I was familiar with that look—shame.

My father let it go. There was nothing he could do, since we were only an hour away from taking the family photo.

About a month later, Ms. Ama was delighted to finally get the finished product to hang on the walls. They were regal, except for the one that included me. I stood in the back, wearing a checkered pink outfit, my lopsided afro matched by my awkward smile. My father wore a sharp dark suit and everyone else was wearing an orange outfit with a big smile. If I had a choice, I would have preferred not to be part of the family photo. I didn't belong. Thankfully, I had only destroyed one picture and the others without me were perfect.

By this time, every night I went to bed with a fresh cut, bruise, or bump and blood somewhere on my body. The fierce pinches were a daily thing either to my ears, my sides, or my arms.

Sometimes she caught me by surprise and sometimes I was aware of what was coming. I couldn't decide which was worse.

Nightly, my fingers searched for the new wound and caressed the scab from an old one; sometimes they were on top of each other. I was broken, living in constant fear and defenseless. I was most afraid on weekends because Ms. Betty and the maids were off and sometimes my father worked or had other things to take care of until late in the day. Ms. Ama was careful to protect her reputation as a good Catholic woman, so she didn't do anything in front of other adults. Still, the maids heard my sharp screams followed by whimpers and sharp warnings from Ms. Ama. They couldn't help me, but they prayed for me and cleaned my wounds in secret. Often, they didn't want to leave me, but they had to.

Every weekend, Ms. Ama would blast country music as we cleaned, and the little children played or watched cartoons. I swept, mopped, scrubbed the floors, tables, and countertops, and dusted the furniture. I also cleaned our bathroom, making sure not to miss a spot.

"Look at this!" Ms. Ama screamed, pointing at something.

My heart rate shot up and my heart began to pound. I didn't see anything.

"Right here, look!" she screamed again in anger, her face flushing red. I froze. She grabbed my left ear with her strong right hand, twisted hard, and pushed my face against the toilet. The speed and force of the push resulted in a slam to the cold, white, round bowl, forming a sizable knot on my forehead and causing pain.

Ms. Ama was undeterred. "I told you to make sure it's clean. You missed this spot!" If there was something, I couldn't see it since I was dizzy from the slam, and the searing pain from my ear, which was bleeding, was screaming for attention. The rest of me was alerted for protection and rescue, since all parts of me were at risk. Ms. Ama reset her hold tighter on my ear, causing another tear, and guided my head to the spot. She pushed my face against it to make sure I saw it. "When I tell you to clean it, you clean it. Do you hear me?" she yelled.

"Yes ma'am," I replied in a choked voice, vision blurred by tears.

She finally let go and walked away.

"God, please help me," I whispered, trembling with pain and fear. "Please help me do this right."

I reached for my ear—it was still there, torn and bleeding, but there. I sobbed for a few seconds until panic set in. I had to hurry before she returned. I grabbed the scrub brush, sobbed and scrubbed. Sobbed and scrubbed. Sobbed and scrubbed. The rest of the day, I was on babysitting duty until I was saved by bedtime. After a shower, I lay in my bed hoping for sleep, but I reeked of Clorox from head to toe. I couldn't focus. I stuck my dry hands between my thighs and took a deep breath. It was a small but welcome relief. I buried my face in my pillow and cried myself to sleep.

"Eliza, come sit with me while I eat lunch," my father called out the following day. I obeyed and sat a couple of chairs down. "We need to spend more time together," he suggested. "Come closer, sit here," he ordered, patting the seat next to him.

I followed his instruction.

"How are you doing?" he asked, smiling and chewing.

"I'm fine," I answered with a nervous smile.

"That's good. Do you like it here?" he asked.

"Yes," I said, after a brief hesitation. I hoped he didn't notice.

"Oh good!" he said, undeterred.

He continued with small talk, but eventually noticed the knot on my forehead, bruises, and bumps on my arms. I was hoping he wouldn't notice my injuries, but I was smart enough to excuse them as products of my own carelessness. He frowned, but easily accepted my explanations. He asked about my life with my mom. I tried to explain as best as I could with my limited English vocabulary, which he seemed to understand given his nods.

"I remember I used to love looking at you in the rearview mirror and you would just look up at me and smile." He laughed in remembrance, then became serious and slowly shook his head.

"Your mother and I were not compatible, but I had a lot of respect for her. She was a good woman. She's a very strong woman and stubborn—oh, and when she got mad, watch out! She would throw plates and things, she was not one to hold back when she was angry! One time, when she was going through the gate at the base, the guard was looking at her legs because she was wearing a miniskirt and she didn't like that. She had nice legs. She came home, put on a pair of jeans, and never wore a skirt again." He enjoyed another laugh from the memory. I didn't respond, just listened and smiled. It was nice to hear him talk kindly about my mother.

Suddenly, he seemed sad.

"I didn't want to leave you there, baby. I hope you know that," he began. "After the divorce I told her we were going back to the states and she asked to spend time with you. I felt bad that I was taking you away from her, so I agreed. I didn't think she would take you. She promised to bring you back by the end of the day and she didn't. I didn't know what to do. I didn't know where to look and I asked my superiors to let me stay until I found you. They let me stay for a couple of weeks, but then I had to go.

Grandma was livid. She was never going to forgive me if I didn't find you," he confessed.

"I'm just glad we found you. Every time we came back I tried. This time, Ama had friends who tracked you guys down," he added.

The news that I was important to both my parents brightened my heart.

But now that I'm here, does he regret finding me?

"This was nice, we should do this more often," my father said. I nodded at him with a smile. "Okay, I have to go back to work. I will see you later." He leaned in, kissed my forehead, talked briefly to my stepmother, kissed her on the lips, and left.

I went back to my room smiling. I finally had some time with him. More time together would be nice. Maybe he'd save me.

I reconsidered when Ms. Ama stood by my doorway—her face flushed red underneath her milky-white complexion.

"What did you talk about?" she asked coldly.

I quickly sat up at the edge of my bed. She was just in the next room when we talked, she could hear everything.

"Nothing," I replied.

"What do you mean nothing?" she retorted.

"He just asked me questions." *Did I do something wrong*?

"Did you talk about your mom?" she asked coldly with her arms crossed. It was then I noticed she was holding a belt in her right hand. My heart began to pound wildly in my chest.

"Um, yes, he asked me what it was like when I was living with her," I answered quietly.

Suddenly, her eyes blazed and her complexion turned beet red as she lifted her right hand and stepped toward me.

Oh God, help me! I didn't move, I couldn't move. I was in shock as she slashed the belt's first blow to the side of my body and it wrapped around my back, followed by another after the recoil. The hits sent shocks to all parts of my body, including my unseen heart and spirit, but I couldn't respond. I raised my hands to reduce the impact of the blows and backed up against the wall. There was no escape. I was trapped in the corner so Ms. Ama was free to do as she pleased and did. Her unrelenting anger toward me was expressed by the belt. It didn't matter what part of the body she hit as long as it landed somewhere, anywhere, and everywhere.

"Don't you ever talk about her in my house! You're worthless like your mother!" she screamed.

I cried and pleaded, hoping for the end. Eventually, she did when Candace came to the doorway, awakened from her nap from all the commotion since I was hitting the walls. Tears welled up in her eyes. *How much did that innocent child see?*

"Mommy," she said, sounding frightened.

"It's okay, baby," Ms. Ama answered, looking back at Candace. "Go back in your room. I'll be right there." Candace obeyed, walking away slowly.

Ms. Ama's gaze returned to me.

"This is my house. Don't you ever talk about her in my house or to your father or you will get it!" she reminded me.

I was terrified, frozen in place.

"Did you hear me?!" she asked loudly.

"Yes ma'am," I said, shaking uncontrollably.

Satisfied, she backed away and left.

I sat on my bed, numb in heart, body, and mind.

What do I do now?

Slowly, my body reawakened from the shock and my shaky hands started to move to sum up the damage. My face . . . my neck . . . my arms . . . my legs . . . my regular tally. I scooted to the edge of my bed crying and was jolted by a sharp sting on my side. I lifted my shirt to find a scratch and a welt the size of the width of the belt. I blinked to clear my watery eyes, to see my arms, chest, neck, and legs—discolored, with raised bruises; every part of my body I touched hurt. My mind raced in panic until it hurt right along with my splitting heart.

I didn't understand, but I didn't regret the time with my father even if it was my last. He cared for me. Hearing that was worth it. Ms. Ama couldn't take any of it away from me. She hated my mother and I represented my mother. Still, I must respect her. This was her home.

"I'm sorry," I whispered, sobbing.

"Go to the bathroom and clean yourself up!" Ms. Ama said, startling me. I didn't even notice she was back, carrying Candace on her hip. I stopped crying as best I could.

I got up quickly to obey. Another round would be unbearable.

Thereafter, I trembled in fear whenever my father came near. I tried to hide when he was around. If he didn't see me, he would forget me, I reasoned. On the rare occasion when he found me and tried to talk or ask me about my cuts and bruises, I pretended not to understand and moved away as fast as I could, trying to excuse myself to a task. The fact that my English was limited, or so I pretended, was helping to save me from more pain. Ignorance was bliss as long as we could all pretend nothing was wrong.

"I wish I could do something," Ms. Betty would say, sometimes rubbing my back in an attempt to comfort me. I wished she could, too. They couldn't help me without losing their jobs and hurting their families. Each morning they came to work, she and the other maid were relieved to see me still in one piece.

At bedtime, I lay in my bed afraid, crying softly and wishing for my mom. It had been too long since I had seen her and Ronnie. I missed her smile, her hair, her smell, her voice. I missed Ronnie, my super-charged protector and best friend. My heart ached for the family I left behind. I wanted to scream, *I don't belong here!* I wished to be poor again with my family, moving from place to place. Those days seemed wonderful now.

I never experienced anything like this. Mom hit us once when Ronnie and I ate some leaves from a tree. She was scared and panicked that they were poisonous. She was crying right along with us, which pained us more than the hit.

Aside from that, the only other time I had been bothered by an adult was when I was about seven years old and an "uncle" had me sit on his lap while he was playing cards and drinking beer with a group of other men. Unfortunately, I was playing nearby with other children nearby and caught his attention. Being an obedient child, I sat on his lap as instructed, but on the edge hoping the request was only for a moment and I could leave. But, once I was seated, he pulled me closer to his belly and I could feel where a bulge formed underneath me. I turned and looked at him, confused and uncomfortable. He smiled and held me tight while he played. His breath warmed the back of my neck. I tried to scoot away, but was too small to jump off without his help. Fortunately, it wasn't too long before my mom came to look for me and ordered me down, all the while, looking at the "uncle" with suspicion. He smiled at her nervously and went back to his cards without saying a word.

My mother was upset, took my hand, and led me away.

"Next time, if someone tells you to sit down on their lap don't do it, okay? Call and tell me," she said.

I nodded. "*Opo*, Mama."

But this kind of punishment in my father's house, I couldn't understand. I prayed.

Am I that bad? What did I do wrong? Whatever I did, I'm sorry!

I lay in bed, staring at the ceiling, whispering between sobs.

It would be better if I was dead. Just as the thought appeared in my mind, I heard just as clearly words from a source unknown.

"No. I'm here, you're not alone." And just as quickly, the voice was gone. I stopped crying. I was scared, and my heart raced. I looked around, but no one was there.

Who was that? Am I crazy?

I had been praying every night to be saved or to see Mom again. I went to Catholic mass every Sunday with my family and I prayed there at the altar, but things just got worse. I was taught to be good and obedient, and God will save and protect you.

God?

I lay back down, scared, but enlivened by what just happened. My heart was refilled with hope—*what's gonna happen next?* I was too hyped up to sleep and had no more books to read. It took a while before I calmed down. I visited Mom and Ronnie in my thoughts. I was with them for a little while.

A New Life

W hen I was little, my father tried to provide for me by setting up a savings account in the Philippines. Though he was thousands of miles away, he made monthly deposits of about thirty dollars. It wasn't a lot of money by American standards, but in a third world country, it meant shelter and food. Mom collected it every month from a bank and worked as a driver to cover the remaining expenses.

Mom, Ronnie, and I lived comfortably in our rented home with food to eat and a few clothes. She didn't have enough to send us to school, but occasionally someone would lend us a book or two to satisfy our curiosity. Unable to read, we looked at the pictures and made up the narrative.

Life was simple. We had each other. We played with other neighborhood kids, enjoyed block parties during holidays or for birthdays celebrations, and on a few occasions, we visited my mother's friends. We rarely visited family members—I believe the "uncle" episode made my mother even more suspicious. We never saw medical professionals. If we got sick, we depended on natural remedies and folklore treatments and extracted our own loose teeth by tying the tooth to a door and slamming it.

"Ronnie! Eli! Come here!" Ronnie and I immediately went running at the sound of Mom's voice.

"I have to tell you guys something," she began as we approached. "We're moving."

"Why? Where are we going?" Ronnie asked.

"I don't know yet. Your father stopped sending money, so we can't stay here anymore. But other people will help us, and we'll be together so don't worry," Mom answered. She gave me no clue as to how she felt about this, or about my father in general. The next day, we gathered the little we owned and began traveling.

"This is just going to be for a little while," Mom explained to her friend who was sitting across from her at the dining room table.

"You guys stay as long as you need to," her friend replied.

We were in the bedroom to allow the adults to talk, but the home was small enough to hear conversations, even those spoken in hushed tones.

"*Maraming salamat*," Mom said humbly. I could tell by her voice she didn't like asking for help or accepting it.

The home was comfortable and modestly furnished with a television, which was a great plus since not many owned one. Mom, Ronnie, and I slept on the floor on sheets with netting over us to keep the mosquitoes from eating us alive. Mom's friends were kind and went out of their way to make us comfortable. We always made sure to help around the house, and stay quiet and respectful and clean to avoid any complaints.

After a few weeks Mom said it was time to go.

"Where are you going to go? You can stay here," her friend insisted.

"It's time for us to go—we've already stayed too long. Don't worry about us," Mom told her.

We moved every few weeks or at the most two months. In time, she had exhausted all her friend options, and had to ask family for help.

Unfortunately, when she left us with her family, she didn't stay with us. Ronnie and I sometimes had to live separately, as well, since most of the time her family members could only take one of us.

In between moves, we would see our mother just long enough for the transition. We enjoyed those short times together and we quickly became used to the drill, so there was no complaining. She reminded us to behave and we never disappointed her.

I was considered different and others let me know it. People were curious about my darker skin tone and my afro.

"Why is your hair like that?" they'd ask, nose wrinkled as if smelling something that stank.

I didn't know. How could I know?

"My father is an American," I finally learned to say proudly, which incited their curiosity even more about America. I found them beautiful, since their skin was a lighter shade and they had "nicer" hair. Ronnie blended in, having lighter skin and large curls like my mom, but I was constantly teased by both adults and children. When Ronnie was around he was my defender; otherwise, I was alone.

I shared their disgust—I didn't like my hair either. I couldn't put a comb through it without pain and it didn't grow down my back, but instead grew upward. I wished I could have their hair and skin, but I didn't, so I just shrugged away their laughs and reminded myself that Mom and Ronnie loved me, regardless. Despite our circumstances and my mother's absence, I never questioned mom's affection and love for me.

God did smile on me, however, with a talent—dancing. Without it I would have lived like a child with leprosy. Filipinos love to sing and dance, and I had my opportunity to shine even if it was just for an hour or two at parties or community dance competitions. Whenever I moved to a new home and was asked, "What do you like to do for fun?" I would always respond, "I like to dance."

Followed by, "Ahhh, show us something," to which I would immediately show them a move or two. I didn't like to dance on demand, and was quite shy, but disobedience was not an option. Thankfully, I always delighted my audience and my ten-second shows always ended with claps and fits of laughter. Dancing was the only time I was appreciated and admired by others, and the word quickly spread. "The black girl, the one with the afro—she can dance really good!"

There was one year when I was lucky enough to stay in one place for about a year. I lived with a distant aunt, her husband, and six cousins—two boys and four girls. Since the home was already full, they accepted me, but Ronnie had to go somewhere else. They lived in a small, sparsely furnished home in a province far from the central city. Everyone slept on the floor, under nettings, and there was no television, but luckily, they had a radio, so we listened to ghost stories tucked in our sleeping blankets every night. The children ranged in age between eight and fifteen, with a couple of them close to my age. The boys were of course the pride and joy of their parents, simply for being males and confident (the adoration probably made them confident). The girls were pretty, with long hair and lighter skin, especially the eldest, who had creamy white skin and long straight hair. Julie, who was my age, had long, dark, pretty, wavy locks, the opposite of the wires sitting on top of my head. Julie's hair was her much-prided crown and it did look like jewelry. Each daughter was unique in their beauty; nevertheless, there was competition.

From the first day I stepped into their home, Julie didn't like me. I was no competition, so I didn't understand why. After the adults finished their questions, had me dance for their entertainment, and excused me to go play, all the children gathered around—including some visiting neighbors who were curious about the new person.

Before anyone could say anything, Julie pointed at me and laughed.

"You're black," she announced loudly, and walked away flipping her hair.

The others stayed, undeterred by her announcement, and continued asking me questions. Julie stopped and looked back, disappointed that everyone stayed without caring what she'd said. She stood far off looking at us and moping.

My other cousins were welcoming, but Julie did everything she could to show her displeasure and snubbed me as often as she could. After a while, I gave up trying to befriend her and focused my attention on the others who were delighted to have me. "Don't worry," they assured me, "she always gets jealous."

Jealous? Of me? That's new.

One day, after winning a dance competition at a community party, I became an instant neighborhood celebrity. I was celebrated by my family, prideful of their cousin who danced so well and won. The neighbors were also thrilled and came over to congratulate us. The rare attention kept me grinning from ear to ear for some time. Julie, however, was not pleased with all my congratulations. She didn't say a word and stood far off, mouth pouted out, staring at me and all the commotion.

"Before you, she was the best dancer. Now, you're the best," one of her sisters confessed.

I understood. I was determined to make her feel better, but the harder I tried, the more she rejected me.

After that, I became popular and easily identified given my afro. Plus, my last name was Jackson, so others entertained that I was related to Michael Jackson. I shared in their fantasies.

"Is he going to come get you?" a neighborhood kid asked.

"Yes, he's going to pick me up in his helicopter," I answered, which was followed by oohs and ahs by everyone listening.

"Ha-ha, you're a negro. Look at your hair, so kinky and ugly!" Julie laughed obnoxiously so everyone could hear. The adults were not around, otherwise she would be in trouble. But I wasn't going to tell, that could create problems. I was just a begging visitor. I took it in, saying nothing back. Every day, at each opportunity, she would repeat her insults.

One day, her insults went deeper. We were in the house playing and she became upset about something I can't remember. "You don't even have a house. You're ugly and your mom doesn't want you, that's why you're here. She can't even take care of you because she has nothing," Julie ranted with everyone looking on.

It was one thing to talk about me, but it was another to insult my mom. My heart pounded, and heat began to rise from my heart to my face. My vision changed, my teeth clenched tight. *Stop—she must stop.*

Instead, she was merciless, repeating the same words over and over again. I reasoned with myself, she was right, I don't have a home. Her words cut me deep. I tried to ignore her and turned my back to play with someone else. Everyone else was quiet, horrified at what they were witnessing and waiting to see what would happen next. They looked at me with pity, which made me feel worse.

Julie wasn't backing down. I turned to walk away and felt a hard push. I stumbled forward and faced her once I regained my balance. She leaned toward me again, arms outstretched, and just as she lunged, I gave in. I grabbed a handful of her long, wavy hair that swung my way and pulled down until she begged me to stop. The other children were now gathered around us and yelling different things. I finally let go. She stepped back crying and looking at me, then rushed to find and tell her parents.

What have I done? Now I'm going to have to leave and my mom will be mad. I shouldn't have done that.

I got scared. A few minutes later, Julie returned with her parents behind her. My heart was beating fast—*will they hit me?* They asked everyone what happened, and they told the truth, including what Julie had been saying for a while. Surprisingly, Julie got in trouble and was spanked by her mother for being disrespectful to my mother for what she said and for making fun of me.

"Don't listen to her. You are family and you can stay here as long as you need," my auntie said in assurance, and hugged me.

"*Maraming salamat po*," I said, as tears filled my eyes for her show of mercy.

Julie was sobbing in the corner for a while, looking at me from the corner of her eyes. Even though she was mean to me I felt bad for her. Thankfully, she never picked on me or said anything mean again. Since we were the closest in age and we had the same interests, it was easy to do things together. We began to have fun. In time, we became close and I enjoyed a short time of peace.

Everywhere I stayed, I was treated like one of their own. Most families had so many children that another didn't make a difference. Our relatives were very poor, sleeping on the floor atop layered covers in the attempt to pad the hard surface and nets over us to protect our flesh from being completely ravaged by mosquitoes during the night. About four to five people were sandwiched together into each netted arrangement, each person hoping no one would be a cover hog.

To relieve ourselves, we went outside to little shacks made of four flimsy walls with a plank of wood as a roof. There were no lights, no water—just a hole that you hoped not to miss when using it or step in while you were trying to find it. Before going in, it was best to open the flimsy door and estimate the steps using as much natural light as possible. A misstep could result in finding your leg deep in human waste. There was no flushing, you just hoped that what was in the hole was far enough down not to touch you, instead of you making a deposit into it. It was a great squatting exercise, plus you learned to go very quickly while holding your breath because of the overwhelming smell.

Many families lived with these accommodations; however, there were lucky ones who had real bathrooms inside their home. For those with bathrooms, after making a deposit or two, a bucket of water is poured into the toilet which swirls the materials down. Flushing with a single touch of a switch was for the rich.

Baths were taken in public at a designated spot for everyone's use. A pump was used to draw water which was poured into individual buckets for bathers. Since it was public, and everyone was there, you washed yourself with your clothes on, being sure not to expose yourself to the men and boys watching and ogling nearby, while cleaning all your body parts as much as possible.

Only the fortunate ones had televisions, so on hot afternoons or on special occasions people gathered around to look through the window of a neighbor fortunate enough to have a TV . . . we would pile up outside and watch. For entertainment, we mostly listened to the radio for music, soap operas, and at night the disc jockey telling a scary ghost story preventing us from even considering getting up at night to use the "shack room." Really, it was best to hold it until light. We didn't have refrigerators, so food was cooked fresh from the market or preserved in some way, but waste was never an issue.

A trip to the market for food was a fascinating and noisy experience, with people gathered in one square area, all shouting, talking, and bargaining for the best deal. Children were running around or hugging their mother's leg for comfort, overwhelmed by all the commotion. There was a pervasive smell of fish and raw meat. Rows of vendor stands sold vegetables, pork, chicken, beef, breads, candies, and local fruit. There was a stand or two of vendors selling apples and oranges for a relatively costly price since they were foreign. Most meals were soup-like, with plenty of vegetables and small pieces of meat, spooned over lots of rice, with a side of salty seasoning to taste. Most of the dishes were made with chicken, fish, or other seafood since they were the least expensive meats.

For fun, we took strolls in the undeveloped forest, climbing trees, picking peanuts, pulling apart sugar canes with our bare teeth, and picking fruits along the way. We swam in the lakes, bugged the bugs, and took naps under large trees. Back home, our stomachs were full of sweets. In the early morning darkness, we sometimes snuck out to pick fruits from the neighbor's tree. Other times we played games like hide and seek, kickball, and hopscotch or danced to music blasting from the radio. We all loved Michael Jackson. Break dancing was very popular, and I was good at it for a girl. With my last name, good coordination, and afro hair, I was reaping the benefits of being different.

No matter the comfort and fun I experienced in my temporary home, I missed Mom and Ronnie every day and prayed for the day we could live together again. Nothing compared to the sight of them, my true home, which came like clockwork.

"Are you sure she can't stay? She's doing good here, where are you going to take her?" Auntie argued. Mom didn't argue, but there was no staying. I said goodbye to as many people as I could and walked away with the few belongings I had gained. When I looked back for one last time, Julie stood next to my auntie in tears. We had come a long way in a year; we wouldn't forget each other.

Burned

During a visit with another relative, my aunt Rosa, she asked us to stay and help since she was about to have another baby soon.

"Do you really need help or are you just trying to help us?" Mom asked suspiciously.

"Well, this way we both win!" Aunt Rosa answered. They went back and forth for a while, but later, Mom agreed with the plan for us to stay.

"They should go to school, too. They can walk together with my kids. It's good for them," Aunt Rosa suggested, smiling, trying not to push too hard and scare Mom away. I stood close to Mom and let out a small gasp of air. No doubt my face lit up at the mention of school.

"You want to go to school?" Mom asked, noticing my reaction.

"Yes, Mama," I answered, smiling, but not too much because it costs money.

"I have some money saved up to get them enrolled and get uniforms," Auntie offered.

"I have some money, I'll figure it out. Maybe I can get another job," Mom quickly replied.

"Okay, we can do it, it will be good for them," Auntie Rosa added, smiling at me and Ronnie. Ronnie and I were thrilled. We would be together again, and we'd get to go to school for the first time!

The following day, Mom, Auntie, Ronnie, and I went to the school to sign up, followed by a trip to the uniform store—white collared top, dark blue overall skirt, and dark blue bloomers for me and a white polo shirt and dark blue pants for Ronnie. Fortunately, our cousins had extra shoes and enough school supplies to enable us to start school in four days. I laid my clothes out two nights before, and woke up very early to make sure I was ready. Our cousins, on the other hand, were not enthusiastic about school, preferring to stay home and play. I put on my clean, sharp clothes, all grins and ready to go after breakfast. Mom was delighted at our excitement, but something was bothering her. Was it about money? I hoped not.

We walked to school about three miles away with the other neighborhood kids, chatting, picking up objects and tossing them, examining small creatures, and salivating at the bakeries making fresh bread, *pan de sal*. No car rides—only rich people had those. The usual modes of transportation were jeepneys, which is a smaller version of a bus; tricycles, which is half motorcycle, half buggy and can fit two adults and two children sitting on their laps; and horse carriages. Mom sometimes drove a tricycle for work.

Once the school bell rang, everyone lined up outside at their designated spots according to class assignment. We placed our hands over our hearts and sang the national anthem with pride.

The school was old and very big, at least from my tiny view. My classroom had rows and rows of desks to hold about fifty students; a large desk with stacked books and a chair was placed prominently at the front center of the room, facing the students. The room was clean, but in need of repair.

"Sit wherever there is an empty desk," our teacher ordered. "Take out your pencils and notepads and we'll begin." She seemed nice, but strict.

Every student was at full attention, especially when the teacher was talking.

"If you have an answer or question, raise your hand and wait until I call you," she instructed in Tagalog. Disobedience was not tolerated, and everyone was expected to pay attention and turn in assignments when due. I loved every minute of learning, but I was behind since I had never gone to school before. I was a quick study, but I had a lot of work to do to catch up. We shared textbooks because there weren't enough for everyone. We had recess and lunch, but for the most part, we stayed in one room with one teacher for our entire learning day.

We had an English class to learn the basics of the language, but most of our lessons were in Tagalog. Most of the teachers were strict, but fair. Respect toward elders and authority was the expectation.

Given my American last name, my classmates assumed I had special experiences. When they asked, I repeated the same story — Michael Jackson is my cousin, he's going to pick me up in his helicopter. Oh, and yes, he will have apples and oranges with him for me to eat.

"Who took my apple?" our teacher asked. "That was a special gift to me." No one said a word.

"If the person who took it does not confess now and I find out who it is, I will not only punish them, but also tell their parents," she added, surely inspiring regret by the guilty party at that moment.

"I took it. I'm sorry," a boy said, head hung low.

"Come up here," our teacher said, waving him to the front of the class as she cleared her desk. The boy stood aside watching, avoiding all eye contact.

"Lie down across this table on your stomach," she ordered. The student did. We all began looking at each other for answers. Suddenly, it was clear. Taking a large wooden ruler in hand, she lifted it midway to the ceiling and quickly back down, striking his bottom.

"One, two, and three . . ." she counted. He tried not to cry, but the humiliation was undeniable. Even though he was at fault, we were sorry for him. After the swatting, he got up, fixed his clothing, and stood still as the teacher reprimanded him and ordered him back to his seat. He did as he was told, wiping his tears away and trying not to look at us. Everyone was on their best behavior after that day, even more so than before.

One day I came home from school to hustling and bustling excitement.

"Auntie Rosa is having the baby," Mom said.

Everyone was busy doing their part to prepare for the new member of the family.

"You wanna go with me to see Auntie Rosa?" my mom asked. "We're going to bring her some soup."

"*Opo*, Mama!" I said jumping up and down, glad to go anywhere with Mom plus see the new baby.

I dressed quickly and sat in the tricycle waiting to go. Aunt Lily came out with the rice soup covered with a towel and placed it between my legs.

"Hold it tight, okay?" she instructed. I nodded. It was a bit warm. Others came out with clothes and other gifts and stuffed them in the remaining empty spaces. Mom came out, said her goodbyes to the onlookers asking her to deliver their messages, and sat on the motorcycle part of the buggy.

"Ready?" she asked me.

"Yes, Mama," I answered, giving her a nod and smile.

"Did they give you the soup?" she asked.

"Yes, Mama, Aunt Lily did," I responded.

"Okay, hang on," she said.

Mom turned on the motor and pushed lightly on the gas. The motorcycle jerked upward then back.

Swoosh. Suddenly, scorching heat covered my body and I screamed. Then silence. Everything stopped. Heat traveled from my chest to my thighs, consuming my skin as it traveled downward. My flesh was burning, causing sensations too severe to comprehend. Mom turned to look at me—her face horrified. She turned the motor off and came to my aid. Everyone else came in a screaming frenzy to help. The soup had just been boiled so it was scalding hot and the rice stuck to my skin, making indentations in my flesh. Mom and the others tried to wipe off the moisture and the rice, peeling my skin off with each kernel.

"Stop!" Mom yelled when she realized what was happening. She lifted me out of the buggy and carried me to a room. She removed my dress carefully, trying not to disturb what skin was left. I studied her face—she was emotional and tearful, but brave and methodical. The pain was dreadful, and I cried, but I tried to brave it—Mom was scared enough.

Soon, a doctor came to check on me. I had suffered third degree burns on my arms, thighs, and chest area. My skin needed to heal in open air and topical ointment, so I couldn't wear any clothes for a while. I couldn't go to school, which hurt more than the burns.

For about three months, I sat in a room wearing only panties, looking out the window as the other kids walked to school each morning and played outside in the afternoons. I was a prisoner in the room, watching other kids live their lives and imagining myself with them. I missed school; at this point I wouldn't even mind a purging event—when we had to drink the thick liquid that made all of us throw up tapeworms during an assembly.

Most of the time, Mom came in to bring me food and smear ointment on my wounds, but if not, Auntie brought it in. In time, I could wear clothes again, but the indentations and scars remained for life. One day, I was thrilled to be free from the room and play again, with the doctor's permission. I mused that maybe I could even go back to school.

"We're leaving tomorrow," Mom told Ronnie and me. We weren't surprised, just nodded our heads. I didn't even bother asking her about school. Moving was our life and school was not a permanent part of it.

The following day, I got ready and waited for Mom to finish talking to Aunt Rosa, who was upset by the news. Ronnie was playing with the cousins nearby. I sat under a tree in the front yard. I fantasized about my father coming to rescue me. He was holding a white dress and bags of gifts in his hands. I ran to him for a hug and he picked me up, giving me a kiss on the cheek. He brought gifts for everyone and handed them out generously to our friends and family. He took me to America in a helicopter and I ate apples and oranges and played with dolls in a dollhouse and went to school every day. If only it were true . . .

"Eli, time to go," Mom called out. I snapped back to see Ronnie approaching, a sad look on his face. He didn't want to leave either. We said our goodbyes, expressed our gratitude for the hospitality, and left with everyone's best wishes and blessings.

Our New Home

"This is your grandmother's house," Mom said.

"Grandma?" I looked over at Ronnie, who was just as confused. According to all my aunts, Mom didn't like Grandma. It was no secret, though Mom never shared as much, out of respect. Mom was honest, sometimes to a fault, and she wasn't one to suppress her feelings. I wondered if I would feel the same way about Grandma. Maybe we were just visiting.

Tap, tap, tap. Mom's knuckles hit the front door. The home was about ten stairway steps above ground; underneath was just open space the same size as the house, enclosed by walls. The door opened, and we were greeted with a huge smile that reminded me of my mom's.

"Oh, come in, come in. I've been waiting for you. I'm so happy you're here." The elderly woman approached, kissing Ronnie and me on our cheeks.

"Hi, Grandma," Ronnie and I said in unison. Mom was clearly uncomfortable—she spoke sparingly and looked a little sick, but she was cordial. She went in and we followed her.

Grandma tried to make the best of it, with small talk to make us comfortable. She offered us food, which was wonderful since we hadn't eaten all day. Aunt Lily told Ronnie and me before we left that our mom hadn't forgiven Grandma for abandoning her as a child to our great-grandmother who passed away years ago. Mom adored her grandma—grateful for her sacrifice—and ignored her mother's existence. It was clear our presence was Grandma's idea. At least we had somewhere to stay, and best of all, we could be together.

"You can stay in here with me," Grandma offered.

"No," Mom quickly rejected. "We'll stay downstairs."

Our grandmother looked worried. "But that's not a place to live. There's no light there, and it's cold. What about the kids, can they stay up here?" she reasoned.

"No," Mom replied sternly. "We're all going to stay down there."

Grandma looked sad, but didn't push too hard. This was the most help my mom would accept.

After our meal, we said our goodnights and headed to our quarters downstairs. Grandma gave us a few candles, frowning with worry. It was dark below, even with moonlight coming in the openings. We couldn't see much, but we managed to spread out our covers and nets and made the hard area as comfortable as possible. Tired from our travels, we fell asleep as soon as our heads hit the pillows. We'd look over our new place tomorrow.

The next morning, I opened my eyes and my mom and Ronnie were still there. I smiled, relieved. I stared at them for a while, joy filling my heart. I sat up and kicked from a tickle on my toes. It was only a small spider, but my heart pounded nonetheless. I scanned our new home—a small open space divided by the home's posts with no lights and no electricity, no kitchen or beds, just a damp dirt floor. The smell of mud and mold were strong; bugs and creepy crawly things made it their home, which we couldn't see last night. It would have made sleeping impossible. Thank God for the nets over us because the mosquitoes alone would have eaten us alive, not to mention whatever else was living with us. I understood Grandma's worry. There were large openings meant for windows or doors, but there weren't any.

"We'll clean it up," Mom said, accurately reading the expressions on our faces. By now Ronnie had awakened to join me.

"Breakfast time!" Grandma called out from outside. She peeked in, still wearing the same frown from last night.

"We'll be right there, we have to get dressed," Mom answered.

"Okay, see you in a few minutes," Grandma said. I sensed relief in her voice.

We went upstairs to eat. Both adults were quiet. Grandma studied us, her face mixed with worry, gladness, and love. She would have hugged us nonstop if Mom allowed it.

Our mother tried to stay away from Grandma as much as possible but didn't limit our time with her. As the days passed, we enjoyed getting to know Grandma, doing chores and helping to make sure we earned our keep.

Afterward, Ronnie and I played outside, sometimes with neighborhood children, in acres of open land until it was night. On days when there were plenty of children, we played kickball and games like tag and hide and seek.

Occasionally, other relatives would come to visit and hand us a few coins, which we immediately took to the nearest store to buy treats, mostly candy. We didn't go to school and Mom was looking for work, so she was gone half the time. When she was home, she would lie down in the hammock outside, slowly rocking and smoking as she watched the sunset. I watched her from afar, wondering what kept her mind occupied.

Once, I was bold enough to ask.

"Nothing," she answered and beckoned me to sit next to her. She was clearly in a far-off place in her mind, a dark, sad place I wished I could save her from. I snuggled in closer, deciding at that moment to become a doctor so that I could heal her—after all, that's what doctors do. Somehow, some way, that was my plan.

After a few months living under our grandmother's house, Ronnie and I got used to living in the cold, damp room even with the moldy smell and bugs. Since we didn't have a kitchen or cooking supplies, Grandma cooked and brought down food each mealtime. Ronnie and I were constant companions since there weren't always other children around. We were well behaved, but managed to get in trouble on one or two occasions.

"Try this," Ronnie offered.

"What is it?" I asked.

"I don't know, but it smells good," he said, caressing the green leaves.

"Okay," I said, putting the leaves in my mouth, copying Ronnie. They had a sweet and bitter taste. We chewed vigorously, looking at each other for any reactions.

"What are you two eating? Where did you get those?" Mom asked, rising from the hammock.

"Leaves . . . from over there." We pointed at the large bush.

Our mother panicked, scaring both of us.

"What? Come here!" she ordered. "Throw it up, throw it up!" We obeyed, sticking our fingers down our throat to gag ourselves, which worked, but it hurt. I hadn't seen Mom so worried since I got burned. After the purging session, Ronnie and I got a spanking with a skinny branch from a tree, a first. She hit me about five times on my butt, but oddly, she was crying right along with us, causing confusing emotions. Ronnie got about ten lashes, harsher, she said, because he was the older one and he was supposed to be protecting me. Being older had its benefits, but more responsibilities.

"Sorry, Mama," we said, once everything calmed down. We didn't like seeing her upset.

"It's okay. I just don't want anything to happen to you, that's all," she answered in a low and sad tone. She beckoned us closer and hugged both of us. We wouldn't do that again.

About a month or two later, Mom came home from one of her job search trips with candy treats and a toy for each of us. We couldn't believe it!

"Your father is here from America," she explained. "He gave me some money and he want to see you," she said, looking at me.

Ronnie looked confused. *Didn't he want to see him, too?*

"We're going shopping tomorrow to buy a new dress and shoes," she added. Father, shopping, this was all too much! I was impatient, anxious for events to unfold. Ronnie and I fantasized about our shopping trip, meeting our knightly father, and life in America until Mom called that it was time to sleep. I didn't have to be encouraged—I closed my eyes tight, prayed, and went to sleep.

I woke up the next morning, heart pounding, and sat up. Was it a dream? I looked over—Mom was getting dressed and urging my brother to do the same. I sat up and she looked over at me and smiled. It wasn't a dream. I got up quickly and dressed. I went upstairs to say goodbye to Grandma, sharing the exciting news and my plans. Grandma was elated. She listened and hugged me close.

"Make sure you pick a pretty dress," she said.

I agreed and joined Mom and Ronnie, who were waiting in the front yard flagging down an unoccupied tricycle. Mom usually was the driver, but today we were customers.

We went to several stores before finding the perfect outfit: a white dress with purple polka dots and a purple bow. Mom picked out white socks decorated with lace and a pair of black shoes. Afterward, we got some food from a vendor and ate so much our stomachs hurt. It was a daydream I didn't want to end.

Finally, we went back home to get ready for the "meeting" next day. Since we didn't have lights, we made sure everything was laid out and ready. I took a pail bath outside, using a lot of soap to make sure I smelled good. I hoped to impress.

This time when I woke up, I didn't have to wonder if it was real. It was in my heart, but I also sensed a sadness I didn't understand. Mom was already awake. She looked tired. *Did she sleep at all?* She sat down next to me, studying and caressing my face. Ronnie was still asleep during this rare moment.

"I talked to your father. You're going to live with him and his wife, along with his daughter and son," she began.

I smiled. "Is Ronnie coming too?" I asked, brightening up.

"No, he's gonna stay with me," she answered.

We've been through this plenty of times. Maybe he'll come later.

"Make sure you behave and listen to your father and his wife. They're nice and they're going to take good care of you. You're going to go to school and I will see you on the weekends. Be a good girl like you always are, okay?"

"*Opo*, Mama," I replied.

She leaned close and hugged me tightly.

There was nothing to worry about; we always came back to each other. She was my permanent home and she would always be there.

"*Mahal kita*," she said. I love you.

"*Mahal kita po*," I said, a huge smile on my face.

We decided it was time to do something with my poufy, coarse hair with lots of help from water and pins. I put on my lovely new dress, socks, and shoes as if it were a ceremony. Once Ronnie woke up and got dressed, we were ready to go.

"Bye, Grandma, bye, Auntie, bye . . ." I said to everyone, giving them hugs. "I will miss you all."

"Here's our address. You write to us, okay?" Grandma said.

"*Opo*." I proceeded to stuff wads of papers filled with addresses inside a small purse Grandma had gifted to me.

After some hugs, tears, well wishes, and goodbyes, Mom and I finally left. Ronnie stayed with Grandma.

I'll see him soon. Still, it was hard to leave him.

Our destination was farther, so after the tricycle ride to leave my grandma's province, we had to take a jeepney. Mom's friend Lucy joined us.

Hours later, it was our stop. I stepped off the jeepney, into a large open space where people gathered and talked. Nearby was a gate with two guards carrying guns. I had only seen this in the movies—soldiers inside a booth, talking to people in cars and allowing them to pass one at a time. It was intimidating, but I felt safe.

"This is a military base," Mom explained. "There he is." Mom pointed toward a stately black man wearing a uniform. He walked toward us, tall and confident.

"Stay right here with Lucy," Mom instructed, handing me over to Lucy.

My parents walked toward each other, met midway, and talked. He handed her a set of keys and pointed to a motorcycle nearby. Minutes later, she returned, took my hand, and walked toward my father. A slight tingle of fear crept in my heart.

My father greeted me with a warm grin, but said words I didn't understand. He had kind eyes and I concluded my mother was right, he was a nice man.

I smiled back shyly, clueless about what to say. My mother stooped down to her knees to look into my eyes. "I'm going to leave you with your father, remember what I said. I will see you soon. Be a good girl," she said.

She asked my father something I didn't understand. He responded, pointing at my things.

"I will see you this weekend," she assured me. I breathed easy. She took all my belongings, including my little purse of addresses. "Your father said you don't need your things. He will buy you new ones. You can use these when you visit us," she said. She hugged and kissed me. "See you soon. *Mahal Kita*." My father, taking my hand in his hand, guided me away. I looked back at Mom, still standing where I'd left her. She waved, I waved back. Did I see a tear? I couldn't be sure. *I'll see her soon.*

The Run

For about a month after my runaway adventure, things were a little better at home. Ms. Ama didn't hit me, but still pierced through me with her eyes. Everything else was the same. After a month of grace, the pinching started again, soon followed by the banging, hitting, and slapping back in full force. I had hoped it would stop, but at least I got a month off.

I continued doing well in school and to my dismay my father lavished praises when he received the reports. I didn't want the attention since they carried a high price, but Ms. Babbitt kept sending messages of encouragement. She was pleased with me, which would have made Mom proud. In private, I paid the price for Ms. Ama's displeasure, but by now I understood that good or bad, everything had a price.

"Oh, great job! My smart baby!" my father praised as he reviewed my report card, which included comments from Ms. Babbitt like "A pleasure to have in class."

"Thank you," I answered, uncomfortable and squirming with my head down as I stood next to him. From the corner of my eye, I could see Ms. Ama standing nearby, arms crossed.

"Come here, honey, look at her report card," he called out to her. She walked over and looked over his shoulder. She didn't say a word. My father couldn't see her face growing dark in anger, her eyes and mouth tightening. His pride angered her.

Please stop! I screamed inside.

She reminded me often that I was worthless, "dumb like your mother," she often repeated. My being clever was not part of her plan. "You are ugly. You have kinky hair and you are black. Your mom can't even take care of you," she would repeat in disgust.

It wasn't anything I hadn't heard before. Julie helped me with that. As punishment, I stopped getting new clothes and in the two years of living in their home, the only toy I ever had was the doll my sister gave me when I first met them.

Fortune graced me again when I met Memory. She was new in our class, but we couldn't be more opposite in looks. Like Cindy, she was strikingly pretty with long blonde hair and green eyes, but Memory was shy like me. She and her family moved in next door. I assumed she wouldn't be interested in being friends with me, but when our family went over to welcome them to the neighborhood, her eyes quickly settled on me and she smiled. It was like an angel smiled at me.

How can someone so pretty like her even look at ugly me?

I smiled back and looked down and away, hoping Ms. Ama didn't notice. Candace went right over to chat with Memory's younger sister, Amanda, Memory's mirror image. Memory came over and stood next to me, claiming me as her friend. I was honored. Ms. Ama looked over at us, confused at our coupling. I agreed—we were an odd-looking couple. She smiled at Memory, shot a quick glance at me, and returned her attention to Memory's mother, who was asking her questions. *Was she saying bad things about me?* I couldn't tell. But after then, Memory and I were inseparable.

Memory and I were compatible in personality and her family was welcoming. Even though I couldn't play, Memory kept me company while I watched the little beauties, becoming a babysitter by association.

"Why don't you go and play with Memory?" my father asked one Saturday. All the cleaning had been done. "You're always watching the kids, why don't you play?"

I looked at Ms. Ama. She looked down.

"Go and play with your friend," he ordered.

"Go ahead," Ms. Ama rejoined, as if surprised I hadn't moved.

Was this a trick?

I went to the bathroom to make sure I looked decent, both excited and scared.

On my way out, Ms. Ama glared at me as she told Candace and Jason to stay nearby so she could keep an eye on them.

I ran next door to Memory's house, hoping she was home.

"Hi." Amanda answered the door, grinning.

"Hi, is Memory home?" I asked.

"Yup," she said, and ran off. Moments later, Memory was at the door.

"What happened?" she asked.

"I can play!" I answered, jumping up and down.

"You can? Yeah, come in!"

Since my younger ones weren't around, I just played all day with my friend. At lunchtime, Memory's mother prepared us ham and cheese sandwiches, chicken soup, Kool-Aid to drink, and two Oreo cookies, which we enjoyed while chatting and laughing. When it was over, I thanked Memory's mother for her hospitality and glumly walked back next door. I dreaded seeing Ms. Ama; she wasn't happy with my play time.

I wished I could stay away...permanently; running away was constantly on my mind. It was time to go. I waited for the opportunity.

"Can you watch *Cujo* with us tomorrow night?" Memory asked one day.

"What's that?" I asked.

"It's a movie about a bad dog that kills people. I can ask my mom to ask your dad," she answered.

"Okay," I agreed. This was it. It would be on a Friday evening, no school the next day. This was the best time so hopefully, Father would say yes.

Later in the evening, I was sitting on my bed reading when he stopped by.

"I told them you can go watch the movie with Memory," he said, smiling.

"Thank you. Is Candace going too?" I asked. I figured Jason was too young to watch such a scary movie, but Candace could be convincing.

"No, she's too young to watch that. You go by yourself and have fun. I told them you can spend the night," he added proudly.

"Oh, thank you," I replied.

Perfect. Easier for me to disappear since they won't be expecting me.

"Well, good night for now." He walked over, leaned down, and kissed my forehead.

"Good night," I said. He was kind. It was going to be better for him once I left.

Next evening, I gathered my things to go. Since it was a sleepover, it didn't look suspicious. I closed my bedroom door and noticed Candace and Jason sitting at the table with Ms. Ama. Candace looked upset, complaining about not being allowed to join me. Ms. Ama looked at me coldly. "You better behave yourself. I don't know why they would want you over. You stink!" she said in Kapampangan, grimacing.

"Yes, ma'am," I responded and walked out the door. *I made it.*

Once safe, I confessed. "Memory, I have to tell you something." I hoped she would understand. Memory looked at me intently.

"What is it?" she replied.

"I have to run away. Today," I said.

Memory's face turned pinkish, and she looked down in sadness. She didn't have to ask why. Her eyes welled with tears.

"Can't you just stay with us?" she asked.

"I wish I could, but I know they won't let me," I answered.

"Can I go with you?" she asked.

"No, your family is good, and they will miss you," I reasoned.

Memory began to cry. "But I'm gonna miss you," she said.

"I'm gonna miss you, too," I replied. "Will you help me?" I asked.

"Yes," she answered slowly.

"Memory, Eli, come in for dinner," her mother called out.

I felt bad. I didn't like betraying her trust.

We went in the house as instructed, but were noticeably quiet.

"You guys okay?" her mother asked.

"Yes, we're just hungry, Mommy," Memory replied quickly, looking away to avoid her mother's eyes.

That night, I had my first slice of pizza, but my stomach was in knots with a million butterflies flying around, so I couldn't enjoy it. I tried to eat, chatting as normally as I possibly could to avoid suspicion. Memory tried her best, too, but it was obvious she was sad. She just kept looking at me as if she had a million things to say.

During the movie, we were both nervous. I hoped no one noticed. About three-quarters of the way through the movie, it was time for me to go. On television, Cujo was still busy on his mad rampage, keeping everyone's attention. I excused myself as if going to the bathroom, then I went outside and Memory followed. We quickly said our goodbyes and I started my journey as she watched with tears in her eyes. I cried too, but my heart pounded louder, and my feet ran faster. When I looked back, Memory was still standing where I left her, but much smaller. I faced forward. Freedom was calling.

This time, I had been invited by a classmate, Rhea, to a "Superman" movie slumber party. She had invited the girls in our classroom and several accepted. Imagine my luck in timing.

Rhea was unaware I was running away, and we weren't close, but she was nice. Maybe her parents would let me stay for a little while. I didn't eat much, I liked to do chores, and I worked hard in school. I had a copy of my report card in my bag just in case. If that didn't work, maybe I could stay at school or maybe some of my other friends would let me spend the night some nights until I finished school.

When I arrived at Rhea's, other girls were already there, and I mixed right in—no suspicion like at Cindy's. We ate, laughed, watched movies, and played games. By Sunday, there was only a few of us left and I got to see Rhea with her parents. Like Memory, they adored her. I wanted to ask Rhea if I could stay, but never got the nerve to do it. Her parents didn't question me staying over another night, and the next morning I went to school with Rhea.

"Eli, please get your things and go to the principal's office," Ms. Babbitt instructed. She looked worried. All the students looked at me, wondering what I had done. So, I did and I got scared. It was a long walk to the office, plenty of time to consider what I must have done. I'd never been summoned to the principal's office before, so the receptionist pointed it out.

I walked into the cold, strongly scented office to find my father and Ms. Ama sitting in office chairs. *Caught again!* Apparently, it wasn't a good idea to go to school if you run away, but there was no way I was going to miss school. *What are they doing here?* I ran away so they could be a happy family and I could find my own family.

"Hi, Eliza. Have a seat," the principal directed softly while pointing to an empty chair. I walked over and sat.

"Eliza, your parents are here to pick you up. They told me that you ran away. Can you tell us why you ran away?" she asked.

I looked at her, my father, and Ms. Ama, and shrugged my shoulders. Ms. Ama looked a little uncomfortable, although she held a straight, proud face.

"Is there something happening at home?" the principal continued. Ms. Ama fidgeted.

I shook my head slowly. It was pointless to say; I would just get in bigger trouble.

"You could tell me if anything is happening. Ms. Babbitt is impressed with you—she says you are a wonderful student," the principal said, smiling and leaning toward me.

I looked down at the ground to keep from crying and shook my head again.

"Okay, well, class is almost over so you can go ahead and go home with your parents," she concluded. My heart dropped. *Back home? But Ms. Ama doesn't want me there!* I screamed inside my head. I slowly got up and followed. I already had my things, so there was no way to escape by excusing myself back to class to get them.

It was a quiet walk to the car. My father looked upset—his forehead wrinkling to the center of his face. No one said a word. We had been here before.

When we got home, I walked into my room and waited for my punishment. Like clockwork, it came in the form of a threat, but not to me.

"If you run away again your father will get in trouble," Ms. Ama said. "The military is very strict. They will take away his stripes. Is that what you want?" she added sternly, waiting for my response. I ran away to stop the unhappiness, not to make problems for him. I couldn't let him suffer because of me.

"I won't do it again," I said, looking down. Satisfied, she walked away.

Coming to America

I n December of 1985, two and a half years after moving in with my father, he was finally cleared to go back to America and I was going with them. Last year, when they went to visit, I couldn't go because I hadn't received all my shots, but Ms. Betty and the maids made sure I had a great time. I enjoyed every minute like I was in Wonderland. After my second time running away, my father asked me if I wanted to go back with Mom. It was meant as a threat, but I answered "Yes" wholeheartedly and started crying, desperate to see Mom again.

I could tell he was shocked and I felt bad about that, but I was tired—tired of my body being torn apart carelessly; tired of hiding; tired of being a toy and a garbage disposal for uneaten food; tired of being a burden and making Ms. Ama mad; tired of being told I was stupid and ugly; tired of having no one to protect me.

I had too many bruises, too many cuts, too many "accidents." She pinched and hit me in places that are normally covered, like my sides, stomach, chest, and back. Each night as I changed my clothes for bed, I could see each point of punishment and I wondered and wept over what I must have done to make her hate me so much.

The "family picture" that hung on the wall was a constant reminder of how different I was from everyone else. *Everyone else could see, why didn't he?* I wanted out, even if it meant giving up my dream of going to America.

It didn't matter if my mom and I were homeless, moving from relatives to friends to relatives. I wouldn't mind just having a few used clothes and slippers and not much food again—we had always survived. I didn't even mind giving up the clean bathroom and having to go in the dark, in the back of a home, dig a hole and go. I could "go" in under one minute and had learned to be careful not to fall into someone else's hole. I would miss school, but I would give that up to for Mom, Ronnie, love, and sanity.

My father was surprised by my teary response.

"I want my mom. I want to see my mom," I sobbed. It felt like forever not seeing her face or hearing her voice. No phone call, letter, nothing. I was sure she didn't have our address or our phone number. *Would my father or Ms. Ama let me talk to her if she called? Would Ms. Ama give me the letter?*

He was stunned. "I'll see what I can do," he said, and ordered me to my room.

I waited, hoping with each day that passed. But nothing happened.

The trip to America was about eighteen hours. I was fascinated and scared being up amongst the clouds, but thankfully it was uneventful. I couldn't believe this day was here. I had been sure they were sending me back to Mom.

It was winter when we arrived in Victorville, California. There was snow on the ground and a gloomy sky to welcome me to America. It was so different from the bright sunny warmth of the Philippines. I was still reeling from the long flight and now I was awestruck by the soft, flaky snow, icy ground, and unbearable cold. I began to shiver uncontrollably. Nothing like this happened in the Philippines. As soon as they were able, Candace and Jason grabbed handfuls of snow, throwing it at each other, and then at trees and objects when they got in trouble. I stooped down and touched it. Cold. Amazing. I took in a deep breath. Fresh. What other beauties would I find in America?

Our new home was temporary, but comfortable. The community was like the one we'd left in the Philippines, with rows and rows of homes and plenty of kids running around playing. We moved into a four-bedroom, single-story home which was cozy, but it was too small for Ms. Ama's taste.

"This is temporary," my father assured her. She winced and let out a sigh.

I had my own room, which I liked. I wanted to be able to read whenever I could find time, but I first needed to find a library. My father was scheduled to work the following week and I prayed I would be enrolled in school by then. Otherwise, I would be alone with Ms. Ama.

A few days later, we went on a trip to see Grandma Betty, Uncle David, his wife Sheryl, and his stepdaughter, Tori, in a city called Panama. On the way there, the freeways were frightening with so many cars moving fast and changing in and out of lanes, coming so close to the dividers. How did they manage to miss the walls? We were only inches away. I closed my eyes until the car finally stopped.

Everything looked bright, expensive, and fresh. All Americans must be rich with all these cars, stores, and stuff.

My grandmother lived in an apartment building about five stories high, only for senior citizens. I was astonished to see so many elderly people in one place all walking around, going up to their apartments, gathering or talking. *Where were their families? That's not how it usually was in the Philippines. Maybe they like it better this way.*

My grandmother's apartment was on the fourth floor and wasn't too far from the elevator. By the time we reached the doorway, Candace and Jason were jumping up and down, impatient to see gifts waiting on the other side of the door. I stood behind everyone, nervous. I was the oddity. *What will they think of me?*

Father rapped on the door.

"Hey! My brother!" A man resembling my father opened the door with a big grin. He looked like a big, tall teddy bear with glasses. My father's face brightened up and he laughed.

"Come over here!" the man said, pulling my father in for a hug. They exchanged greetings before Uncle David focused his attention on Ms. Ama, who was standing next to my father.

"Ama! My favorite sister-in-law! It's good to see you!" he said and gave her a hug.

"Hi, David. How have you been?" she responded softly, accepting his embrace.

By now, Candace and Jason were vying for attention.

"My babies!" he said. "How are my precious ones doing?" he asked, hugging and kissing each one.

They happily told him they were fine.

"David, let them in," a woman's shaky voice called anxiously from inside the apartment.

"Oh, I'm sorry, come in, I'm hogging up all the attention." He laughed heartily.

We all entered the cozy apartment as people exchanged greetings. I stayed quiet. A small kitchen was just to the right of the entry, followed by a living room with a patio and one bedroom with an attached bathroom. The smell of cleaning products was strong, along with something else I didn't recognize.

My eyes immediately focused on an elderly woman sitting in a blue oversized recliner chair wearing a pink and white nightgown and white slippers. Her hair was gray, short and curly. She wore glasses and had the kindest eyes I had ever seen. She looked just like my father. She must be Grandma. Next to her was a cane and a tray with a pitcher of water. Next to the recliner chair was a small couch where two other people sat—a lady with shoulder-length curly hair and light cocoa-colored skin, wearing a nursing uniform, and a teenage girl wearing stylish clothes, with dark hair just below her shoulders.

"Eli, come here, baby," my grandma said, reaching for me. I approached, feeling a bit awkward. Should I stand in front or next to her by the side of the chair?

"Give me a hug," she continued, smiling longingly. I followed her lead.

Is she crying? When I looked again, she was wiping her eyes.

The room was quiet.

"I can't believe this," she said. "My prayers have been answered," she continued, tears falling from her eyes and rolling down her bubbly cheeks. She hugged me while reciting her fears. Unexpectedly, a hand was on my back.

"Yes, it is wonderful to have her with us again. Thank you, Heavenly Father," Uncle David praised. Everyone was staring at us with a variety of different expressions on their faces. Candace and Jason looked confused—what was the big deal about me? My insides were squirming, but outside I stood still, frozen. Uncle David hugged and kissed my forehead tenderly. I was moved by his kindness, but my tears were mixed with fear because Ms. Ama was surely going to get me.

When Grandma let me go to greet her other grandchildren, Uncle David introduced me to Aunt Sheryl and Tori, who were eagerly smiling, but with their foreheads wrinkled. *Were they sad or worried?*

"It's nice to meet you," my aunt said. They looked at me intently and hugged me tightly. I nodded and smiled. I answered their questions as quickly as possible. My heart raced, and my mind rambled about the upcoming punishment for all this attention. *How do I escape this ambush?* I wished it would stop and my mind started racing in desperation for a solution. I excused myself to use the bathroom. Inside, I shook in fear. *What am I going to do?* Once I got up the nerve, I went back to the others to avoid suspicion.

When I returned to the family room, I retreated to the corner of the room by the patio, hoping to be unnoticed. For a while the conversations flowed—the adults were eager to catch up on each other's lives.

"Where's Eli?" Uncle David asked.

"She's over there in the corner," Aunt Sheryl answered quickly, but almost in a whisper.

Uncle David looked over, frowning in confusion.

"Come here, Eli," he gestured toward him. I got scared. I looked over to Ms. Ama, who avoided my eyes and looked away. I walked over to him, scared stiff.

"What's wrong? Why are you sitting over there and not with everybody else?" he asked. His voice sounded pleasantly concerned.

How do I answer that question?

I shook my head.

"Come here." He sat me next to him on the couch and looked into my eyes, which were now welling up with tears. He hugged me tight.

"It's alright, baby," he comforted. He couldn't possibly know why.

"Can I talk to you for a minute?" Aunt Sheryl asked Uncle. He nodded, and they stepped out of the apartment. A few minutes later, they returned.

"Okay, brother. Let's get some alone time together," he said jokingly, but seriously.

"Okay, brother, let's go," my father answered, a little subdued. "We'll be right back," he said to Ms. Ama as he leaned in and kissed her cheek.

"We'll be back, Mama." They both kissed my grandmother and left. Aunt Sheryl sat next to me with Tori on the other side. For the first time in a long time, I felt safe. Aunt Sheryl distracted me with a gentle barrage of questions. Ms. Ama sat nearby, watching and tending to the little ones, but often looked my way. Candace and Jason were vying for Tori's attention since she was the "cool" teenager, but she didn't budge from my side.

When my father and uncle came back, they had a surprise.

"Okay," Uncle began, "Eli is going to come and live with us for a while," he said.

Ms. Ama looked stunned, but didn't say a word.

I was stunned too. *Does my father not want me anymore?* I looked over at Aunt Sheryl; she didn't look surprised.

"Oh, that's nice," Grandma said, smiling.

"Well, that way she can help you out and spend time with you, Mom. She can go to the school down the street and come over to help afterward," Uncle David added. My father was unusually quiet with his head hung low, avoiding the four sets of eyes staring at him for answers.

"Yeah, that's right, that's good, I can use some help and we can spend time together," my grandmother said, clasping her hands together.

"Can I stay, too?" Candace asked.

"No!" Ms. Ama responded abruptly. Everyone was quiet for seconds too long.

"Well, Mom, we're gonna go, we have a long ride home. I'll see you soon," my father said, leaning over to kiss her goodbye.

"All right, baby, I'll see you guys soon," she answered.

"We're gonna go too, Mom. I'll bring Eli back in the morning to visit you," Uncle David said, leaning over to kiss her, too.

"Okay," she responded. "I'll see you tomorrow."

New Family

D espite my shock, I looked forward to living with Uncle David, Aunt Sheryl, and Tori. My prayer was answered— no alone time with Ms. Ama. It was a quiet ride home, but there were whispers between the couple. I looked out the window, still amazed at all the things to see. It was all so different from the Philippines.

We arrived at another apartment complex, where my eyes immediately settled on a small cement pond of blue-green water highlighted by lights beyond gates with several signs posted on walls around it.

"That's a pool," Tori explained. "But we can't go in there until summer because it's too cold. Do you know how to swim?" she asked.

I shook my head no. I had been in shallow waters in the forest and waded in at the beach, but nothing like real swimming.

"I'll teach you," she offered. I smiled in agreement.

Inside, their home was modestly furnished and decorated, with three bedrooms and two bathrooms. It was clean, but there were spaces with clutters, piles of papers, and miscellaneous things I didn't recognize.

"This is going to be your room," Uncle David said as he showed me to a bedroom and turned on the light. There was a bed and dresser, but there were piles of clothing and other items on it, as well as on the floor. Uncle David started clearing the items into a box and I started to help, but Aunt Sheryl interceded. "No, baby, you go sit down in the living room, we'll clear this up for you. We didn't know you were going to come with us today or else I would have cleaned it up already. We'll get this place looking nice for you in no time," she assured me, smiling. I smiled back. I didn't care about the room, I was just glad to be there. In an hour, I had my own room, but no clothes.

"Don't worry, we'll get you new clothes," Aunt Sheryl said.

"I have some clothes I don't wear anymore I can give you. Plus, Christmas is coming up so you will get presents." Tori shared this with a grin before going in her room to search for giveaways.

Uncle David was kind, with an infectious, hearty laugh. He had served in the military during the Vietnam War, and worked for the local transportation system as a bus driver. He was an ordained minister for the Methodist Church, too, following the path of my grandfather, who had been dead for twenty years. Uncle David held services on Sundays at a small building in Panorama City; about fifteen people attended each week. He didn't get paid for his work, but he was faithful and used his own money to maintain the church.

Aunt Sheryl was about five feet tall, with a curvaceous body, kind eyes, and a soothing voice. This was the second marriage for both of them. A registered nurse who'd put herself through school despite a difficult childhood, she enjoyed being a pastor's wife and the parishioners were drawn to her warm personality. She was just as committed to building the church as Uncle David; both of them were passionate about helping people in need. Because of the size of the church, there was no choir, but they put together the music weekly. It was a true partnership and they worked well together in service of others.

Cousin Tori—fifteen years old, with a petite womanly build like her mother—was attractive, witty, and charming. Tori was Auntie Sheryl's only child and unfortunately, Tori's father hadn't been a part of her life since Tori was very young. Her father's absence and a poor relationship with her mother ex-husband caused her to be detached and unwilling to trust another man, which made it difficult for Uncle David to be her father.

Tori was smart, but school didn't interest her. It was difficult at times to gauge her mood, which changed from day to day; her highs and lows made her difficult to approach at times. She and her multitude of friends were always the life of the party. She had many boyfriends and admirers—too many to count. But, given her temper, she also got into a lot of fights at school and parties due to jealousy from others over guys. People flocked to her and she loved the attention.

A few days after I moved in with them, Tori offered me a new role.

"Eli, come here," Tori called. I walked over. "Help me clean my room and I can give you some clothes," she said, smiling. Her room hadn't changed since the first time I saw it. She was the luckiest girl in the world, but clueless of her fortune. Her clothes and things were piled on the floor and on top of her dresser. She had so many clothes, shoes, scarves, and purses, and so much makeup and jewelry—everything a girl desires—and they were everywhere. I stood by the doorway. It was impossible to walk in or around the room without stepping on something.

"Come in, come in," she waved, "it's okay if you step on something," she said, sitting on her bed surrounded by even more clothes.

"My mom said I had to clean my room or she wasn't going to get me anything for Christmas," she confessed, pursing her lips. She leaned over to turn on the radio—saying she liked it loud for "motivation"—and then sat back down.

I looked around. Her walls were plastered with posters and pictures of artists like Prince and New Edition.

"I've been meaning to clean, but I just hate to. My mom said it's just too much now. I need to give some of this away. If you see anything you like, let me know and we'll see if you can fit it," she said, making the offer enticing. I liked the plan, since I didn't have much and she had such nice clothes.

But where do I begin? Tori noticed my confusion.

"Umm, just stack up the clothes, the clean clothes on that side and later we can put them on hangers," she answered. Second problem, the clean clothes were mixed in with dirty clothes, so I had to ask her about every single item I picked up as I put them in separate stacks. She picked up a shirt here and there and put them away, but the look of the room didn't seem to change. She might as well have just left them on the floor.

"Do you have a boyfriend?" she asked. I frowned and shook my head shyly. "Of course not," she said teasingly. "Your uncle is not going to let you have one, anyway. But you're cute, mixed—a half breed, so boys will like you," she said.

Me, cute? Half-breed? That was the first time anyone had ever called me that. *She's just being nice.*

"Oh, let me tell you about this guy—" she began, glad to have a willing audience. She talked about everything, her friends, boyfriends, admirers, parties, activities nonstop while I sat on the floor sorting. I loved to hear about her dramatic life—it was like my own soap opera.

Occasionally, she would come across something that was too small and give it to me. By the end of the day, I had a nice pile of clothes. "It's so much easier when someone helps me and keeps me company," she said, keeping her gaze on me for a response.

"I'll help you any time you want."

"Great! Thanks!" she said, smiling.

A few weeks later, Uncle David finally received my school records so he could enroll me in school, so that weekend, he took me shopping for new clothes at Gemco, since Aunt Sheryl and Tori had hair appointments.

"Go ahead, pick out some clothes," he said, smiling. I was thrilled and a bit overwhelmed. I picked out underwear, socks, dresses, pants, and tops. At Payless Shoe Store, I picked out a pair of pink and white tennis shoes.

After the shopping spree, we went to eat at In-N-Out Burger. I chose a cheeseburger, fries, and a strawberry shake for my first meal at an American fast food place—it was delicious!

"Uncle, how did you meet Auntie?" I asked, once we sat down to enjoy our meal.

"Oh, Auntie, she's a good woman. Very smart," he said proudly. "Everybody loves her at work. She's a very good nurse. Unfortunately, when she was young her stepfather was abusive to her. Didn't care nothing about her, treated her like she was nothing and she had to fend for herself. Her mom loved her, but didn't help her. She had a stepbrother and stepsister, and those were his kids, so he took care of them. But her, uh-uh. It's a shame. When she turned eighteen, he kicked her out of the house, so she had to take care of herself. And now, she always helps them out when they need it. Her mom passed away and she really misses her. Sheryl could do anything—she's that smart and determined," he added.

"What about Tori?" I asked.

"Sweet girl. Now she's smart, too, but she doesn't apply herself. She's too busy with other things and boys and gets distracted. She should be focused on school and her grades, but she doesn't and she's always getting in fights because girls are jealous of her. At first, we got along well like a father-daughter, but I tried to help one day when she and Sheryl got into it and Tori felt like I betrayed her trust, so after that, it never was the same. I adopted Tori, so she's my daughter—that joker, her father, was never involved in her life and she suffered for it. She wants to have a father and I want to be her father, but Sheryl won't allow me to be that. She doesn't want me to discipline her or anything, she wants to do it. But she's too lenient on her. Part of that is because of what happened to her when she was growing up. She doesn't want the same thing to happen to Tori, but I wouldn't do that. She's fed up with her behavior, but she won't let me help her."

He paused.

"I love Tori and I want to help her, but they won't let me. A lot of our fights are because of that. She's out of control. I don't have any children of my own and to me she's my child, in my house," he said solemnly. "Oh well, maybe one day. But I have you now," he added, smiling.

I smiled back. To me, he was a father . . . a good father for me and Tori.

"Okay, Eli, we are going to the beauty shop to do something about your hair," Aunt Sheryl said the next day. "I can't believe they let your hair get like this. Ugh, it's just terrible," she continued.

She took me to a beautician and requested a wash, deep conditioning, relax, and style. "If they just took care of it, she has pretty hair," the beautician said, shaking her head.

"That's all right, we'll get it in shape in no time baby." Aunt Sheryl smiled at me.

First Tori called me cute, now they are saying I can have pretty hair? They're just being nice.

What seemed like half a day passed sitting in the chair or under the dryer until she was done.

Finally, "So what do you think?" the beautician asked, pointing me toward the mirror. Aunt Sheryl stood beside us, smiling.

It took me a moment of staring into the mirror to realize I was looking at myself. My hair was parted on the side, loosely curled, the ends hitting my shoulder. I turned my head to look at the sides.

"Ooohh, look at you, so pretty," the ladies teased. I looked down, feeling a flush rush to my cheeks.

"I'll bring her back in two weeks," Aunt Sheryl said to the beautician.

"Okay, see y'all then," she responded. "Take care of your hair, pretty girl," she added causing me to giggle and flush even more as we left the salon

Like clockwork, every two weeks I went to the beautician, who washed, set, and put me under the dryer for style. I liked it, but my mixed-race scalp couldn't tolerate it.

When I lived with my father, I had to wash my hair every day, which Aunt Sheryl said had damaged my hair. She said I had black hair and you can't wash it every day like that. Being half Filipino, my hair became oily faster, but Aunt Sheryl insisted I only wash it every two weeks. By the second week, I was suffering. My head itched so bad my scalp was raw from me scratching.

"It's so itchy," I told Aunt Sheryl when I was brave enough.

"Just put some of this on it." She handed me a jar with a smiling lady's picture on it.

"Okay," I said, taking the jar and following instructions. Instead of improving the symptoms, adding grease made it worse—my hair became too oily and weighed down. Eager to please, I didn't say anything else. After all, she was taking care of me. I couldn't win. One day, when I could, I would take the middle way.

"You should take a bath," Aunt Sheryl said. "You're always taking a shower. You're a young lady and ladies take baths," she added, joining me in the bathroom. I looked at her and she must have noticed my confusion. I had never taken a bath. Ms. Ama always had me shower.

"First, make sure the tub is clean. If not, then clean it out." I looked at the tub—it had dirt marks all around the edge. I grabbed the Comet and scrubber and quickly cleaned it. "Now, push the stopper down and let the water run," she instructed. We watched as the water rose to the mid-level of the tub and then she turned it off.

"Okay, now get in, sit down, and wash yourself," she said, leaving to give me privacy, closing the door behind her. I took off my clothes and got in, careful not to fall. I sat down. I grabbed my washcloth, soaped it up, and began washing my arms and worked myself down, but the soap rinsed off the cloth once it hit water. Now what? I stood up, re-soaped, and washed again, trying to stay balanced. I sat back down, rinsed, and the water changed color; particles were floating around. *Yuck, I'm sitting in my own dirt, how am I supposed to get clean?* I let the tub water out and soaped the washcloth again, washing Filipino style and rinsing with a large cup of water. *There, now I'm clean.*

It was wonderful not to be responsible for anyone else. I played, read—did whatever I desired after finishing homework. I helped around the house—cleaned, washed the dishes, swept the floor, vacuumed, and cleaned the bathroom—everything except for cooking, which Auntie did most days after work. Tori didn't like to clean, but she helped with cooking.

Christmastime, I had plenty of gifts—clothes, shoes, books, a purse, and Barbie dolls with accessories. It was unbelievable after how I had been treated at my father's. Tori received just as much, but was ecstatic about the cassette tapes from her favorite artists.

Tori seemed to enjoy being a big sister, giving me clothes that didn't fit anymore and taking me places just for fun on the rare occasions when Uncle David allowed it. She had multiple admirers plus a rebellious spirit, so Uncle was skeptical about allowing me to go with her for fear of boys being around.

"Where's Tori, it's six o'clock," Aunt Sheryl asked one school night after arriving home from work.

"I don't know," I answered.

"Get in the car," she commanded. I didn't hesitate, scared that something bad happened to Tori.

A few minutes later, we pulled up to a house and Aunt Sheryl strode to the front door, still wearing the white pant suit that was her nursing uniform. She knocked loudly at the door and a minute later, a young man opened it.

"Where is Tori?" she asked sternly. Shocked, the young man pointed toward the back of the house.

"Tell her to get out here now," she demanded.

The young man turned quickly and minutes later, Tori came outside, holding some pieces of clothes and her purse, her clothes disheveled. Aunt Sheryl grabbed her by the arm and rushed her to the car. Both of them were screaming, and Tori was crying.

"He is nineteen years old, you have no business with him. I can call the cops on him!" Aunt Sheryl threatened.

"We weren't doing nothing, just watching TV!" Tori insisted.

"Oh really, who do you think I am, Boo-Boo the fool? You were supposed to be home hours ago," she added, in a rage. They argued back and forth until Tori gave up, arms crossed, sobbing and pouting.

Once home, Tori rushed to her room, but Auntie was right behind her, belt in hand. I had never seen Tori get punished before. The door slammed behind them. From my room across the way, I could hear the belt slap against flesh.

The sound was too familiar. I shivered.

Tori screamed for mercy. "Mom, stop. Okay, okay!" while Auntie Sheryl yelled at the top of her lungs. Not long after, Auntie left Tori alone in her room, but not before telling her she was grounded for a month.

About two to three times a week, when his schedule allowed, Uncle David picked me up from school, took me to eat at In-N-Out Burger or El Pollo Loco, and dropped me off at home before going back to work. I immediately started my homework and played outside with friends after I was done. Later after dinner, I washed dishes and then prepared for the next day. The days Uncle David didn't pick me up, I walked to Grandma's house to spend time and help with chores.

After months of living with them, my hard work and discipline earned me new nicknames from Auntie and Tori.

"You're a Goody Two-Shoes," Tori teased.

"She's the Golden Child," Auntie followed.

I didn't respond. *Obedience makes me weird.* They didn't understand me. *I don't understand the American way, either.*

I didn't understand disrespect and disobedience or taking parents for granted—especially when I longed for mine. Tori and I were opposites in personality: strong-willed versus obedient. She got in trouble a lot and I didn't. Uncle argued to be included in disciplining Tori, but Auntie wouldn't allow it—she said he was too strict.

Tension rose in the house.

On days Uncle David didn't pick me up, I was instructed to call Auntie Sheryl as soon as I arrived at Grandma's house, but I sometimes forgot. A few minutes after missing my appointed time, Auntie would call my grandmother's apartment to make sure I had arrived.

"You didn't call again like you're supposed to," Aunt Sheryl said, by my third time.

"I'm sorry, Auntie, I forgot," I confessed.

"Well, I'm gonna have to talk to your uncle so that you can stop forgetting," she said and hung up the phone.

What does she mean?

Later at home, Auntie approached Uncle, demanding he punish me as a reminder. The request turned into an argument.

"Spank her for what? She was there at my mom's, wasn't she?" Uncle offered. *Spanking?* I shook.

"You are too lenient with her. I have to punish Tori for what she does, but you don't punish her," Aunt Sheryl argued. That was all I could understand before I tried to muffle the noise with my pillow. I sat in my room, scared from all the yelling.

Then suddenly it was quiet.

A few minutes later, Uncle came into my room, slow and defeated, holding a large brown belt in his right hand, and closed the door behind him.

Oh no! My heart jumped, and fear set in. *It's happening again!*

"I'm sorry, baby, but I have to spank you for not listening. From now on you have to call your aunt as soon as you get to Grandma's," he said softly.

I nodded my head vigorously.

"Lie down on your stomach," he said. I obeyed. He gave me ten whips, but I cried much harder from a broken heart than the lashes.

When it was over, I sat up on my bed, my face tear-stained. Uncle was upset as he walked away and closed the door behind him.

"I am never doing that again!" he told Auntie on the other side of the door. She didn't argue back.

It was a quiet dinner, all of us avoiding eye contact. My world had shifted again, I just didn't know how much.

Before I lay down in my bed that night, I kneeled to pray. I felt closer to God since moving with my new family, so I asked for forgiveness for my disobedience and asked for his protection over all of us. I had faith He would listen, He had saved me, after all.

One evening, Uncle David came home and announced, "We bought a new house."

"Where?" Tori asked.

"In Heather Hills," he answered.

Aunt Sheryl was quiet. Tori and I looked at her for a reaction. Nothing.

"Is it big?" Tori asked.

"Yes, there are four bedrooms, a living room, a den, and a nice sized yard," he answered.

"When are we moving?" Tori asked.

"In about a month," he answered.

Tori and I were elated about the news, but Aunt Sheryl's silence was disturbing. Why wasn't she excited, too?

Days later during an after-school lunch, Uncle David confessed. "I was trying to surprise her—I thought she'd be happy. But I was wrong. And it's too late now, I already put down the deposit. She's right, I should have included her," he added sadly.

Aunt Sheryl wasn't satisfied, but not long after, we moved.

The home, built in the 1960s, was large, divided into three levels with four bedrooms, three bathrooms, a living room and den, and a two-car garage. On the first level was a guest bathroom with a toilet and sink, followed by the den. About ten steps up on the second level was the living room—the largest wall covered up with medium-sized tile mirrors with gold line etchings. A sliding door led out to a covered patio, followed by a small backyard that led up into a hill. Good for hiking, but not for playing.

The shrubbery was overgrown, with patches of both live and dead grass and weeds. On the side of the yard was a storage shed I wanted to claim as my playhouse until the gardener said a snake had already claimed it. I gave up on that idea and on playing in the backyard altogether.

All the windows and doors had steel bars for protection. From what? I had no clue.

"It's so old," Tori commented. Auntie winced in agreement.

"Well, we can do some work on it," Uncle offered.

"I wanted a house I didn't *have* to fix," Auntie quipped in a huff.

It was the first time she voiced her feelings in front of everyone.

Uncle didn't respond.

Tori and I had our own rooms. Auntie's sister Suzanna moved into the last bedroom, and the three of us girls shared a bathroom.

After the move I went to a new school near Grandma's house called Vena Elementary. I walked to Grandma's house after school to help out. I made sure she ate and took her medication.

Uncle's work schedule changed so it was a rare occasion when he picked me up from school. I enjoyed spending the afternoons with Grandma. Sometimes her friends would come over for discussions. They gathered in the living room and talked about religion, current events, philosophy, and their shared memories. Sitting at the dining room table, doing my homework, I listened and occasionally looked up to watch them. I enjoyed hearing stories from these wise, gentle women.

After homework, I washed dishes and cleaned the kitchen, then sat on the floor next to Grandma and watched television or listened to her stories, while she played with my hair. Her soft touch and voice soothed me, made me drowsy, and sometimes I fell asleep. In the early evening, Uncle or Auntie picked me up. If it was early enough, I would go outside to play until the street lights turned on. Uncle and Auntie fought at times—unlike my father and Ms. Ama who never argued—but nothing scary. My contributions around the house were appreciated.

Life was simple.

On my birthday, I received plenty of gifts, but the most memorable was a Precious Moments Child's Bible with my name inscribed in the front.

"This is your first Bible," Aunt Sheryl said proudly.

"It has my name on it," I said, my heart feeling full for the genuine expression of love.

"Yes, it does. It's all yours," she answered, as they all looked at me proudly. "You can read it whenever you want, and there's a study guide you can follow," she added.

"Thank you for everything," I responded and gave them both a hug in gratitude.

Since we attended church every Sunday I grew to learn more about God. He had to be the One who whispered to me when I wished for death. Now that I had my own Bible, I read more and more, curious about this God who had rescued me.

I began my spiritual journey into understanding the unconditional love of God and Christ with the guidance of my guardians. I was too young to understand Catholicism when I was in the Philippines, but one difference I was relieved to find was that Easter was celebrated differently.

My first Easter in the States, I didn't know what to expect, but was surprised when Auntie took us shopping for new clothes for the big day. On Easter Sunday, church was followed by an Easter Egg hunt, then a celebratory dinner to honor Christ's rising from the dead.

Where was the long parade of men dressed only in pants and thorn crowns, their faces covered in handkerchiefs, who flogged themselves with a whip, drawing blood that splashed and trickled down to the ground? Or the tumblers who threw themselves to the ground, bruising and cutting themselves? Where were the men who dragged heavy crosses for miles or the one who was hung up with ropes like Christ was long ago? It was explained as honorable by my family, but as a child, it was terrifying to see. When I slept the images turned into nightmares.

School continued to be energizing. I only had one semester to prove that I qualified to move to the seventh grade and not get held back. Although my English was limited, and I was behind, I worked hard and earned mostly As. Math was more difficult for me—yet another language, so sometimes I got Bs or Cs on math quizzes and tests.

Ms. Cole was my new teacher. She was patient and understanding, but firm. She loved to eat raw broccoli, which made her breath smell. Every time she got close the broccoli was intensely present. Nevertheless, we all liked her and held our breaths as long as we could when she talked to us, exhaling once she moved on.

"You're doing well, you're gonna get it," she assured me when I was challenged. I was her little foreign experiment; eager to learn, eager to please, I received good marks despite my challenge in fluency. My accent was still very heavy, so it was difficult at times for people to understand me. I still read constantly and turned in extra credit book reports, which Mrs. Cole praised me for.

Thankfully, I became close friends with another Filipina girl, Naya, who was in my class. She was quiet and reserved, like me, but I think we became friends instantly because of our shared ethnicity. She spoke Tagalog, which made our conversations easier and our bond stronger. Naya had an accent, too, but she was way ahead of me in English. During recess, it was easy to figure out what to do since we had the same interests—handball and kickball—or we just sat and talked. After school, we walked home together with other pre-teens going in the same general direction, and at a point, she continued with her brother and cousins while I walked the other way, usually by myself.

Every year, the school held a talent show. Individual students performed, and each classroom also performed a dance or an act. The sixth-grade classes performed a group dance and song, Whitney Houston's "The Greatest Love of All."

"So, is anyone going to perform in the talent show?" Ms. Cole asked, smiling, after an announcement over the intercom by the school principal encouraging students to participate.

Everyone in class giggled, and "No way!" was the general response.

"Oh, come on, I know you have talents. You are the leaders, you should be brave and set a good example for the younger students," she reasoned.

The class, in general, continued to giggle, joke, laugh, and shake their heads in protest. Ms. Cole just smiled. "Okay, well, if any of you change your minds, just let me know, we'll sign you up," she said.

"I'll do it," I said at the end of class when everyone was gone.

"Oh, really? Great, I'm so proud of you!" she said, clapping her hands together in delight. "What are you going to do?"

"I'm going to dance," I answered.

"Wonderful, you're gonna be great!" she said. "I'll put you on the list right now," she added, smiling.

"Thank you," I said and left the classroom.

What did I just do? Everyone will be watching.

Naya was waiting for me and I told her about it during our walk. She looked at me, listening and smiling. Then, suddenly, she burst out laughing. Now I was really scared. Once she calmed down, she tried to be encouraging, but it was too late, I was already petrified.

When I got home that night, I asked Tori for help.

"Oh, wow!" she said cupping her hands to her face. I waited for her to burst into laughter, but she didn't.

"Of course I'll help you. We can pick out the music and put an outfit together," she continued, busying about like a personal planner, looking at cassette tapes in her collection and listening to each one. "Prince, Michael, Janet! What have you done for me lately?" We began singing and dancing together.

Uncle and Auntie were proud of my courage. Tori assembled my trendy outfit and critiqued my routine, but the rest was up to me. I watched the music video when I could and tried to copy some of the moves, practicing every day and enjoying every minute.

Even Grandma was enthused for me, and occasionally she would ask me to do my routine, which sent her into fits of laughter.

"You're a good dancer," she would say, clapping her hands and laughing.

The day of the talent show, my heart raced, my palms were sweating, and it was hard to sit still. I had already gone to the bathroom to pray earnestly for deliverance. I really hoped God was listening.

"Attention all students, after recess, please report to the auditorium for the assembly. Your teachers will tell you where to report," the principal announced over the intercom before recess.

"Okay, class, after recess go backstage in the auditorium to get ready for the show. I'll be there waiting for you. Good luck and I'm so proud of all of you!" Ms. Cole said. My stomach turned into knots. I couldn't even eat my snack.

After recess, we all piled into the auditorium and went to our designated spots. The principal started the show with a few words, and then wished everyone well. The first performance was a group song from the graduating class, followed by class performances, beginning with the kindergartners and progressing to the top class. Afterward, the individual performances began. One by one, students showed off their talents—singing, dancing, reciting poetry or speeches. They all turned out well, which gave me some hope—except I was flushed, sweaty, and my heart wouldn't calm down.

"Please, God, help me," I repeated over and over again.

Before long, it was my turn.

I took a deep breath and walked to the middle of the stage where the spotlight shone brightly. I wore a long, pink-collared tuxedo shirt wrapped with a black belt, black Capri tights, pink socks, and oxford-style black shoes. I stood, posed, and waited. I heard the crackling noise—the tape was rolling. I hoped they had put the right one in. My song started, and I moved. Immediately, I forgot the crowd, my fears, and everything else. I felt different—confident, clear, and powerful. I made not one misstep. The nervous energy was gone, my heart and body were warm. It was just me and the music, alone, until it stopped. I froze in my final pose.

The whole assembly stood and applauded in a frenzy, and it seemed to last forever. The noise had awakened me back to reality and I started to blush and feel shy again. I bowed and walked backstage to Ms. Cole, who hugged me in pride. My classmates congratulated me, and some even said they wished they performed, too. I wished Mom and Ronnie could have seen me and could enjoy this moment with me.

"Thank you, God, for helping me," I whispered, floating on clouds. I was thankful, but also glad it was successfully over.

A month later was our sixth-grade graduation and it was the last day I saw Naya.

Although things were lighter at home, I longed for Mom and Ronnie. Many nights, I prayed and cried myself to sleep, wondering how and what they were doing. Seeing Auntie and Tori together made me long for my mom even more, and it upset me whenever Tori was disrespectful. She didn't understand her good fortune.

I couldn't even see my mom and relied on pictures in my head. Often, I allowed my mind to wander, taking long strolls with Ronnie and our friends, doing as we pleased with freedom. Everything here seemed closed off, fenced off, prohibited by something or someone. I was blessed by my experiences, but I missed my mom and brother terribly. Not a letter or a word from them and I was clueless on what I could do. I asked Uncle and Auntie, but they didn't know either. Realizing my torment, Auntie Sheryl suggested signing me up to see a therapist for counseling, but Uncle David decided that church and prayer would suffice.

When summer began, I went to a week-long summer camp which reminded me of the Philippines since we explored nature. It was an exhilarating experience, bunking with so many people, singing by the campfires, and competing as a group. When I returned home, I spent the rest of my vacation days with Grandma while Uncle and Auntie were at work. Tori went to summer school or spent time with her friends. Uncle picked me up in the early evening as usual to take me home. One day, during our drive back, he was unusually quiet. He and Grandma had talked earlier, and it looked intense. He seemed defeated.

"You know that I love you, right?" he asked.

"Yes, Uncle," I answered, feeling suddenly uneasy.

"We love having you around—all of us. But your father wants you back, and Grandma agrees with him. She says that you are his daughter and you belong with him. I told her I did not want that," he confessed, "but he has a right."

I was stunned. *Don't I have a right?* I couldn't believe what I was hearing. My heart was sinking deep in disappointment, and then deeper in fear. I started to cry.

"Do I have to go?" I asked in panic, tears dropping off my cheeks and onto my lap.

"Baby, give your father another chance, he wants to make things right with you. Your aunt and I will always be there for you. He and Ama said that they're going to treat you right and if they don't, just tell me, okay?" He spoke with tears his eyes.

There was nothing more to say and when I got home to my room, I cried myself to sleep. That weekend, I packed my clothes and things, and looked at my room one last time as my uncle took my bags to the car. Then we were off to Victorville—to my father, the little beauties, and Ms. Ama. Wondering what was in store for me, I looked out the car window silently.

I'm Back!

U ncle and I arrived at my father's house in the early evening. Candace, Jason, and Jay were anticipating our arrival, looking through the window. They started jumping up and down, mouths and eyes wide open, once they spotted us. Once we were close enough, they ran out to greet us with hugs and kisses. My father was close behind them.

"You're gonna stay with us?" Jason asked, eyes bright and a big smile on his face. Candace and Jay stood next to him, all expecting my response. I looked at their irresistibly adorable faces and sensed a sincere welcome. I smiled back and nodded my head yes. The jumping resumed until our father urged us to come inside.

Inside, I greeted my father with a hug.

"Hi, baby," he said, holding me for a few seconds.

Uncle busied himself with his other niece and nephews, then greeted his brother warmly.

"Let me show you your room," Candace said as she grabbed my arm and led me further into the house. My heart sank, but Candace and Jason's warm touch comforted me.

I stepped into the formal living room, which was nicely decorated as expected. In the kitchen, Ms. Ama was feeding Lacey, who was wriggling impatiently in her high chair. Lacey was adorable, with a round face, fair skin, and teary big eyes. She was upset and pleaded to get down and be part of the commotion with her siblings. She stopped when she saw me.

"Hi, Ms. Ama," I said softly.

"Hi," she responded. I got goose bumps on the back of my neck.

"Come on, let's go to your room," Candace insisted, and we were back in motion up some flights of stairs.

"Here it is," Jason announced joyously. All three of them studied my face for a reaction.

"Thank you, it's nice," I said, trying to look as joyful as I could. Once again, the jumping ensued, along with fits of laughter. Adorable.

I entered the room, which had a bed, nightstand, and dresser. Across the hallway was the bathroom. Jay sat on my bed as Candace and Jason busied themselves with putting my things away. They told me how much they'd missed me. I could hear Uncle laughing and talking to Ms. Ama down in the kitchen.

"Kids, come on downstairs so we can eat!" Ms. Ama called.

"Coming!" Candace called back down as we all made our way down the stairs. I picked Jay up and carried him on the side of my hip to save time. He stared up at me with his big brown eyes, his arms wrapped around my shoulders. Grandma loved his eyes and always fussed over his chubby cheeks. He hugged me trustingly as I carried him downstairs, bringing warmth to my heart.

As always, Ms. Ama had cooked a delicious meal which everyone enjoyed, especially Uncle, who didn't usually get to eat sweets. The adults chatted openly about a variety of subjects, including David's home life.

"I don't know what I'm gonna do with Tori," Uncle confessed. "She's out of control and Sheryl just refuses to let me discipline her," he added.

"Hmmm, that's a tough one, brother," my father answered.

"Why didn't they come?" Ms. Ama asked in a stern voice.

"Oh, Sheryl had to work," Uncle answered.

"Hmmm ..." my father and Ms. Ama chimed. Her smile looked more like a smirk.

After dinner, Uncle David and my father left for a while to have their "private time." I was hoping when they returned Uncle would say he'd changed his mind and I was going back with him.

"Okay, everyone, I'm gonna go, I gotta go to work in the morning. Come here, my little sweeties," he said, as he bent down and opened his arms wide. They ran over and jumped into his embrace. I stood aside and watched. My face got warm as tears blurred my vision. I sniffed quickly to stop the flow. *Don't upset the little ones.*

Finally, Uncle looked at me and came over to where I was standing. He put his arms around me, hugged me tight, and kissed my forehead.

"You're going to be fine, baby. You're going to be fine," he said.

I whispered a prayer to God he was right. Tears were coming, but I held them in. No need to upset the babies, I'd cry later by myself when I lay down to sleep.

"It's going to be different," Ms. Ama said to me after we finished cleaning the kitchen for the night. I didn't respond — what should I say? I managed a smile. I wondered how, but for my sake, I hoped it was for the better.

For a while, it was true, things were different, and I was thankful. I was enrolled in a nearby middle school to begin the seventh grade. I became friends with a classmate who reminded me of Naya, and I even had a little more variety of foods in my lunch box.

About two months later, things were back to normal.

The good news — she didn't hit me anymore. *What's stopping her now?*

The bad news—her words were even crueler. And my diet of oatmeal and toast for breakfast, with peanut butter and jelly sandwiches, apple juice, and raisins for lunch, was back. I ate what I could but sometimes opted to go hungry rather than throw up.

I stayed faithful to the idea that Mom, Ronnie, and God loved me. I read my Bible every night before I went to sleep. The Bible said we would go through hardships and instructed us to keep the faith because God will help us through it. I braced for help and lost myself in books and school. At the end of the semester, we were on the move again, this time to Las Vegas—their chosen place for retirement from the Air Force.

On my first day at O'Dell Robertson Middle School, I was in awe of how fresh, new, and big it was. The classes, including PE, were indoors because of the hot temperatures, which get as high as 115 degrees during the summer. The temperature inside was well regulated to ensure comfort; the classrooms were clean and orderly, and the cafeteria was huge. It was exciting to start over, like in books, and I looked forward to seeing where this new adventure would take me.

It wasn't long before I met a petite bubbly Filipina girl when I sat next to her in my first class. She had long, shiny, straight black hair, a bright smile topped with dimples, and sparkling eyes to match.

"Hi, I'm Lindley," she said, smiling and looking at me with eyes precisely darkened by eye liner and lashes fan-shaped by mascara. She smelled of a sweet perfume and every time she moved her long hair, a different fresh scent was released.

"Hi, I'm Eliza," I answered. God's grace, I met my new best friend.

Lindley was smart and talented in so many areas (including an awesome singing voice) that she found it difficult to focus on school matters. She reminded me of Tori. One interest she focused on was a blond-haired, blue-eyed boy named Lenny—she told me she'd had a crush since they met years ago.

"Oh my God, isn't he cute!" she proclaimed.

I looked over, trying to see what she saw in him, but I couldn't, so I just shrugged while she looked at him dreamily.

Lenny had a twin brother, Jake, who was just a tad smaller in build than his brother. She loved to be around Lenny, and flirted incessantly with both, but she didn't ignore any of the other cute boys who passed her sight. It was entertaining to watch her fuss over boys, but I didn't share in her adventures. My sights were set on getting straight As, but she did give me a window into romance as she talked and sang about past, current, and future, full of life and fantasy. I relished being in her company since she helped me forget my life's troubles. Her life was my live soap opera, like the ones Ms. Ama watched all day.

The move to Las Vegas was a welcome distraction for Ms. Ama as she busied herself in reconnecting with other Filipinas married to military men whom she'd befriended over the years. She took pride in creating a comfortable home, with all-new furnishings to show her good fortune. When she had visitors, she quickly introduced me as her stepdaughter, wearing a look of embarrassment as if I were a dirty rag. The other ladies were nice; some even looked at me with pity. But once she was in the other room with them, she spoke in low tones, almost whispering, with a look of disgust. I knew she was talking about me.

After some time, my new friend Lindley grew persistent about spending time together outside of school.

"Just ask her. Maybe she'll say yes, you never know," Lindley insisted.

"Okay, okay, I will," I agreed to make her stop asking.

One Saturday afternoon, I was brave enough to ask, trembling from nervousness.

"May I go over to Lindley's house?" I asked.

"Who is Lindley?" Ms. Ama asked in a matter-of-fact tone.

"My friend from school," I answered.

"Hmm. No, you have cleaning to do. You don't have time for that," she answered coldly. I was not too disappointed, since I had expected it, and scurried away as fast as I could. There, now, Lindley can leave me alone about it when I tell her on Monday.

"Well, I'm going home with you today," Lindley announced, smiling, to my horror.

"What? No, my stepmom will be mad," I argued.

"Well, she won't let you come over to my house so I'm going to yours. It won't be that bad, you'll see," she decided as we walked home. I admired her bravery, but it would cost me. "God, please help me," I whispered.

Luckily, when we got there, my father was home, sitting in the living room. Saving grace.

"Thank you, God," I whispered.

"Come in, come in," my father said, getting up to meet Lindley at the door.

"Who is your friend?" my father asked.

"This is Lindley," I answered.

"Well come in, precious," he said, beckoning her in. "Come sit down," he added, genuinely glad to see a friend of mine.

"Thank you," Lindley said, smiling as she entered in full confidence even at the sight of Ms. Ama. She sat down to join my father in the living room. Ms. Ama looked at her as if she was a stray—not welcome in her house.

I sat next to Lindley and worried about Ms. Ama while my father and Lindley exchanged jokes and stories.

By the end of the visit, my father adored Lindley.

"Come back and visit again sometime, Lindley," he offered.

"Okay, I will," Lindley responded teasingly, intensifying Ms. Ama's obvious displeasure. I walked her out and she burst into giggles once we turned the corner of the street.

"See, I told you it would be okay. But your stepmom is mean!" she said, eyes widening.

I looked down, knowing that somehow it must be my fault. We reminisced over the event until it was time to hug and go our separate ways.

"Ugh, what kind of friend do you have? Those clothes she wears and all that makeup, like a prostitute! I don't want her in my house," Ms. Ama would later tell me while my father was busy watching television. I listened, but it was no different from what she said about other women—they were all "whores." I was relieved my father liked Lindley.

The day the school year ended, my father sat me down and told me I was going back to live with Uncle to help with Grandma, who had gotten sicker. Ms. Ama looked disturbed. It was the best news, but I was sad about leaving the little ones and Lindley, whose bravery was rubbing off on me. I couldn't use the phone to tell Lindley, and I was not allowed to go to her house, so I prayed to God to keep her safe.

I was ready to go and the summer break from school made it the best time for the transition. Uncle came to get me, brightening our home again and bringing me great joy. I was saved. He enjoyed my stepmother's hospitality, complete with great-tasting food and delicacies and a bag of treats for the road.

"How come Sheryl never comes with you when come visit us, David?" Ms. Ama asked, although her tone gave away that she already knew the answer.

"She had to work," Uncle answered casually.

"Hmm," she replied, judgelike.

It was pretty clear that Ms. Ama and Auntie Sheryl didn't like each other. They kept their conversations to a cordial minimum and stayed away from one another as much as possible.

After the brothers' private talk, we packed the car with my belongings and began our trip back to California. I was full of smiles, my joy only dampened by the sad faces of the little ones as they hugged me tight and pouted to tears before we finally drove away. It reminded me of the day I left Mom, except I had no idea our time apart would be so long. There were still no letters or the sound of her voice through a telephone even though I wished it every day. *Why did my father have to take my stack of addresses?* I would have written to Mom and Ronnie every day.

Summer Crush

"You're gonna go to Panama Junior High, that's close to Grandma's house, and you can walk home after school when I can't pick you up," Uncle David said during our trip home.

I secretly wished it was Porter Junior High where Naya went, but anywhere away from Las Vegas was fine.

"Grandma really needs help, she's not doing too good. I told them we needed you back so you can help. I don't know what happened when she was staying at my brother's, but she hasn't been the same since she got back. When I asked her about getting you back here, she didn't even argue about it. She said okay," he added.

Grandma was my father's greatest advocate and Uncle accepted it since he had been favored by my grandpa.

I hadn't confided what I went through with Ms. Ama with anyone, including my uncle, but he and Auntie were disturbed by the pictures that hung on the walls—particularly the one that included me. One day, that photo disappeared during one of Uncle's visits, never to be found again.

I recalled Grandma's short stay with us at my father's house, but I was in school during the day. She needed around-the-clock care after another stroke that had rendered her immobile and completely dependent on others for her basic needs—bathing, eating, hygiene, and to ensure she took her medications. She was bedridden and couldn't go to the bathroom on her own, so others had to clean her. Grandma was proud and hated having anyone clean her—enough to wish she was already in heaven. That's probably the reason she stopped taking her medications sometimes.

Staying at Uncle's wasn't a good plan for Grandma after the stroke since he and Auntie had to work. Ms. Ama was at home during the day, so it was their best plan for about three months. Grandma never complained to me, but she did look sad. She didn't feel good and didn't like being a "burden," I knew that much. After school and before starting my homework, I sat with her when she was awake to share my day and stroke her hair like she used to do mine. Ms. Ama was often upset and whispered things under her breath in Kapampangan when she left Grandma's room after cleaning or feeding her, but that behavior was normal to me. At first, the complaints were low, but after time, they became louder. But I never imagined Ms. Ama would mistreat Grandma.

"She didn't tell me too much. Grandma's not one to talk about anybody, so it doesn't surprise me, but she was just not the same. She seemed sad when I went to get her, but she was so happy to be back. She appreciates Sheryl more," he said.

"Grandma told me she was sorry and that I should bring you back here," he added. Why would Ms. Ama be mean to Grandma? That was contrary to Filipino values.

Finally, I was safe to tell Uncle my story. I was ashamed and felt tainted by my experiences. I said it must be my fault Ms. Ama didn't like me, but I didn't know how to fix it.

"It is not your fault," he argued. "Children should not be treated that way. I am so disappointed in my brother," he professed, "He should have protected you. I don't know what's going on with him. Our parents raised us better than that. That's okay, baby, you don't have to go through that again. As long as I live nobody's gonna touch you like that again," he assured me when we arrived home.

I still had my own room, but it was half full of stuff since it had been used as storage. Auntie's sister, Suzanna, had gotten married to a newly ordained preacher and moved out to begin her new life. Prior to that, she was unsatisfied with her lifestyle and decided to change in hopes it would change her fortune to mirror her sister's success.

I was safe again. I reorganized my room to make it comfortable. Since it was still summer break, I spent most of my time outside, playing with other kids in the neighborhood or swimming at Auntie's friend's apartment complex. I became friends with a pretty biracial girl named Chloe, who had long, spiral curls and big brown eyes with long eyelashes. She was tall and shapely, and wore braces. The braces had to be tightened every month or so and during those times, she said it was so painful she couldn't eat. She was energetic, with a songstress voice, and she loved to dance as much as I did. She was self-conscious about her weight—always talking about reducing it, with the urging of her stepmother. We spent much of our spare time together, but sometimes she hung out with the older "in-crowd" teens in the neighborhood, trying hard to fit in.

"Are you going to summer school?" Chloe asked one day.

"No," I answered.

"You should go, I'm going, it's gonna be fun!" she added.

Uncle had mentioned that he wasn't going to send me to that school—Feldman Junior High—even though it was right down the street, but maybe he would, just for the summer.

Later, during dinner, I dared to ask Uncle if I could go. Auntie supported it and Tori chimed in with her agreement. After a minute or so, he agreed it was a good idea, so I would have something to do during the day. I was elated. Most of the kids in the neighborhood were going, to have something to do and avoid boredom.

The school wasn't like O'Dell Robertson—it was rundown and badly needed repair, but the young attendees were well dressed, wearing brands like Nike, Guess, and Adidas. I was clueless about brands, I wore whatever was bought or handed to me. I had no idea that my "Pro-wing" brand shoes from Payless Shoe Store were uncool.

The first day was invigorating; these students were full of energy and spoke out freely. The ethnic makeup was primarily blacks, some Hispanics, and a handful of Caucasians. It was different being around people my shade or darker and they looked at me strangely, especially when they heard me speak. My accent was still as thick as fog and I mixed words around or used them out of order and pronounced them differently. Chloe introduced me to a few of her friends before she disappeared that morning— thankfully they were nice.

When the bell rang and school was over, I was a little disappointed. Chloe was right, this was fun, and the energy in the halls was intoxicating. I walked through the hallway toward the spot where Chloe told me to meet her, and then, unexpectedly, Cupid struck. About fifteen feet away, walking in my direction in a crowd of students, was the handsomest boy I had ever seen. He was average height for boys, skinny, with tan skin and short curly hair. My heart jumped—I couldn't take my eyes off him.

"Oh, that's Alex," a new friend said, waking me from my stupor. "He's in the drama club. Why? You like him?" she asked coyly. I smiled and blushed. "Really?" she asked, unimpressed. She looked at him again, her nose turned up.

"Well, he does drama and all that, so nobody likes him like *that*, but he's nice. He's just so little and scrawny," she said.

I didn't care about her opinion. I was glad to like him all by myself.

The next day, I stood at the same spot, hoping to see him again. This time, he was walking with other students.

I revisited the idea of going to Feldman during the regular school year with my uncle, but he didn't budge. I dropped the subject to avoid further suspicion since I was only fourteen and not allowed to have a boyfriend until I was sixteen. When summer school ended, I said goodbye to my new friends, and though we had never met, I secretly said goodbye to Alex whom I regretted I would never see again.

"Where have you been?" I asked Chloe when she decided to stop by. I hadn't seen her in two weeks.

"I had cheerleading practice," she answered. "Maybe your uncle will let you do it, too. You can come to practice tomorrow to see if you like it," she invited.

"Cheerleading? What's that?" I asked.

"You'll see, you will like it," she added, smiling and shaking her bosom.

I agreed to ask.

"Can I go to cheerleading practice with Chloe tomorrow? She said I might like it," I asked at the dinner table.

"Cheerleading, that's good. You'll like it since you like to dance," Tori responded, reminding my aunt about my sixth-grade talent show.

"That would be good for you," Auntie seconded.

"Sure," Uncle David answered, "go. And if you like it I'll think about it."

Tori went on to share her experiences in cheerleading, but I wasn't sure it was for me. But since Chloe was always busy, my late afternoons and evenings were spent watching movies like *Weird Science* over and over again with Tori's cousin, Katrina, who was a frequent visitor. So I figured I had nothing to lose. Katrina decided to go with me since she had nothing better to do.

The following day, Chloe's stepmother dropped us off at a nearby park. We approached a group of girls, two of whom were a little older and stood in front. Chloe excused herself and joined them. Katrina and I stood on the side, watching with other onlookers. Once they started practicing—dancing, tumbling, and chanting—I was sold. Katrina decided to ask her mom, too.

When practice was over, just as we were about to leave, a group of boys passed by and one of them was Alex. My heart stopped.

"Who are they?" I asked Chloe when she came over to us.

"Those are the football players. We cheer for them," she answered. Interesting, I thought.

When I got home, I was worked up about joining the team and immediately told Auntie and Uncle I wanted to be a cheerleader.

"Oh, that's good. You'll have fun," Auntie answered.

"Hmm . . . I don't know about that," Uncle responded.

"Why not?" Auntie asked.

"I don't like what they wear—those short skimpy skirts. I'm a pastor and she's a pastor's kid. That would not be setting a good example," he said.

"I can't believe this. Why did you let her go then? And why was it all right for Tori to do it, but not her?" Auntie argued.

"Well, I changed my mind," Uncle answered coolly.

"That makes no sense," she said, walking away. She was clearly upset.

The argument didn't end, however, it just continued behind closed doors.

"She's my niece and I make the decisions for her," I heard him say through the door.

"You have to let her do some things. You can't just keep her cooped up in the house," Auntie pleaded.

"I already made up my mind," he finished.

I was upset. I couldn't believe it. I wasn't allowed to go to parties, to the movies, talk on the phone, visit family members in Los Angeles, or go to events like concerts. He was so protective of me, it was like living in a cage while watching others live life. I asked again, but there was no changing his mind.

Frustrated, I called Grandma to ask if I could stay with her, explaining what happened.

"Of course, you can, baby. I'll have a talk with your uncle," she said.

"Thanks, Grandma," I said.

I gathered some of my things to go. Uncle was unmoved and drove me to Grandma's house. It was a quiet ride. He dropped me off and I ran inside.

"It's all right, baby, I'll have a talk with him. But you can always stay here," she assured me with a hug. We talked until it was time to go to bed.

Grandma told me a story about her oldest son, Stewart, who ran away as a teenager and never came back because my grandpa was very strict. It broke my grandma's heart so much, she didn't have another child until nearly twenty years later. When she did, she told Grandpa that this time she was in charge. He didn't resist.

I slept on a roll-up bed next to hers, comforted by the closeness. Sometimes, I watched her sleep, watching her chest rise and fall, mouth slightly open, her all-white hair thin and pinned up at the top of her head. She was a perfect grandmother.

For nearly a week, I stayed at Grandma's house. By week's end, Uncle was sitting in the living room talking with my grandmother when I arrived home from playing outside. I went to the bedroom to give them privacy, but I managed to hear a little.

"David, you have to let her do things and give her some freedom. She can't just be in the house all day. She's almost fifteen—she's growing up. I let you do things like playing football and joining the band when you were growing up," Grandma reasoned.

"Yes, you're right, Mom," Uncle answered softly.

Whatever else Grandma said to him, Uncle agreed to let me cheer, and the next day I went back home.

The following week, I went to practice with Chloe. My build was good for cheerleading—petite, flexible, and coordinated. I learned to deepen my high-pitched voice for the chants, and worked on the exacting routines.

When we were chanting or dancing, I slipped into a zone. Here was something else I was good at, and I didn't mind performing in front of the crowd since I was part of a group. The cheerleading and football squads consisted mostly of the girls and boys from

Feldman, and they flirted and socialized whenever there was a chance.

I was disappointed to find out that Alex didn't make the team (which was coached by his father) and so he had to settle for the next squad down because of his smaller weight and size. Nevertheless, I was thrilled to be accepted by the cheerleading team and learning something new.

I wished Mom could come and watch me like some of the other parents did. I wished I could see her and Ronnie, period, but I thanked God for the blessings I'd received thus far.

Ninth Grade

O n days my aunt and uncle couldn't pick me up, I took the bus and then walked two miles home, by myself. The bus carried interesting people—some were scary and at times, looked at me weird. I tried to ignore them and avoided eye contact. None of my friends accepted Uncle's logic as to why I couldn't attend Feldman; I explained I had to take care of Grandma, but they didn't believe it. Auntie and Tori didn't understand it either.

"She's not going to Feldman and that's final!" Uncle insisted.

"Ugh, you make no sense," Auntie answered, defeated. It was a lost cause. I let it go, grateful that at least he still let me cheer.

I was nearing fifteen years old, and should have been in the ninth grade, but I'd only completed half a year of sixth grade and a full year of seventh grade. Uncle and I were both disappointed that I was a grade behind—not because of failure, because I was a straight-A student, but due to technicalities. Uncle was supposed to enroll me in the eighth grade, but he formulated a plan—a long shot, but would be worth it if successful.

"I'm going to register you in the ninth grade since I don't have your records. Because of your age, they will believe that you should be in the ninth grade. But it will be up to you for this to work. You will have to keep getting good grades so by the time they get it they won't want to send you back," he reasoned. I agreed, and we moved forward with the plan.

Panama Junior High School consisted mostly of Hispanic students. Boys attended the school too, but Uncle was more optimistic about me being around Hispanic boys than black boys. I fit right in and quickly made friends. I earned straight-A grades as planned, but I decided I needed to be active in extra activities, too. I didn't hide—in fact, I made it a point to get to know teachers, school staff, and administrators. I won second place in the Spelling Bee contest, joined the Honor Society, and when asked by my teacher, agreed to enter my art project in the Los Angeles County School Art Fair. I would have joined the drama club to add to my resume, but I had missed tryouts the previous year and my thick accent would have been a detriment.

About twice a week, I went to Grandma's house when I didn't have cheerleading practice. The other days, I walked to the bus stop, took a twenty-five- to thirty-minute ride sitting next to another student for company until her stop, and then walked the rest of the way home. For safety, I avoided walking past certain homes where it seemed that every day there would be men waiting for girls to pass by and trying to lure them in a conversation.

"Eliza Jackson, please report to the office," the announcer on the classroom intercom commanded. Everyone looked at me, some with soft whispers of "Ooooh." My heart pounded all the way to the office.

"We received your records," the administrator began. "This says you only completed the seventh grade. You didn't complete the eighth grade," she finished.

I shrugged. "But I'm fourteen . . ." was all I could manage.

"We'll figure it out," she responded calmly. "You can go back to class."

I couldn't leave the office fast enough and I hurried back to class.

"Please help me, Father," I whispered in prayer, standing outside my classroom. Just as soon as I whispered the words, I knew it was going to be okay.

"Your school called me, and I talked to them," Uncle told me after school. "They decided to let you stay in ninth since you're doing so well—they would be crazy to send you back. Anyway, it's official, you've been promoted to the ninth grade," he added, laughing. I joined in his laughter and hugged him. The scholarship awards, citizenship awards, service awards, and my activities had all paid off.

Saturdays were game days and halftime was our time to perform and entertain the crowd. Our football team was undefeated, so celebrations happened weekly, but I couldn't go. Sundays were routine—up at 8 a.m., grab a quick breakfast, and then get ready for church. I liked going, but dreaded having to wear nylons (one of Auntie's rules of "being a young lady"). They were itchy and hot especially in the summer, they squeezed my legs, and the crotch part never fit right. After dressing, I tried to squeeze into the bathroom to brush my teeth and sneak a peek in the mirror to make sure my face was clean, but that was always a battle amidst Tori's beauty preparation, which usually entailed the radio blasting, curling iron heating, and makeup and toiletries scattered haphazardly all over the bathroom counter. During the week Tori played popular music, but on Sundays she played gospel music, which pleased Auntie and Uncle.

The church service usually lasted about two hours in our small congregation, with music led by Uncle and Auntie. Uncle's message provided hope and love, but he also hinted at urgency, to motivate people into action. I enjoyed listening to him and often wondered if Grandpa had taught the same way. It was obvious that Uncle enjoyed preaching, especially since he didn't earn any money for it and used part of his work wages to keep it going.

"One day, I'm going to be in ministry full time like my father," he would say. That was his dream.

Sundays also included a trip to Furr's Cafeteria after church. The buffet-style restaurant offered so much food I salivated imagining the roast beef, vegetables, meat patties, fried chicken, and fried okra. I would think hard about it in advance, strategizing about what to eat first to make the most of the trip. The lines were usually long, but it was always worth the wait and Uncle enjoyed making small talk with the hostesses who waited on us.

Once football season was over, most of my time was spent on studies and preparing events as the newly voted district youth church president when Tori stepped down to focus on school. I did well all around but did get into some mischief even when I wanted to do what's right. I was love-struck, and I didn't know how to control it. It consumed me even as I fought it. I took the bus home when Uncle couldn't pick me up, but one day, he decided to follow me—right to Feldman, where I was visiting with Alex in the parking lot.

"Get in the car!" he ordered me, enraged. Dismayed and embarrassed, I understood what Tori felt like when Auntie dragged her out of her boyfriend's home years ago.

I was scared, too—shocked and confused. Alex looked a little scared, too. Alex and I had never touched, hugged, much less kissed or held hands. Being in his presence or hearing his voice talking about non-sensical things that had nothing do with me or us was enough. He wasn't my boyfriend, but I shouldn't have been there.

I was busted.

It wasn't a quiet ride home. Uncle had lots of questions along with some choice words for me. I listened quietly and answered when prompted. For the remainder of the year, either he picked me up from school or I went straight to Grandma's house. I was devastated, but I understood his position.

Sometimes I called Alex from Grandma's house when she allowed me to use her phone—I huddled in the bathroom and talked as low as possible. Grandma never asked questions. Our conversations were so innocent, mostly me listening to him talk about his day, what happened at drama club or football. He rarely asked about what was going on with me except to ask what happened the day Uncle came to pick me up. I saved him small sentimental gifts and notes, hoping for the opportunity to give them to him one day. I wanted to be obedient and stay away from him, but somehow, I couldn't. Mom would have been disappointed. God, too.

Throughout the year, Tori was busy catching up on school credits so she could graduate, but she spent the rest of her time with her boyfriend, Kamel. Kamel was over six feet tall with a muscular build and smooth dark brown skin. He was handsome and had a curl—a popular hairstyle at the time—along with a great sense of style and plenty of charm. Genuinely kind, he was a favorite of my aunt and uncle. Kamel and Tori were inseparable, but they argued a lot. Tori was strong-willed and Kamel tried to please her most of the time, but they fought passionately, breaking up every other month and then getting back together. They couldn't stay away from each other for long.

Kamel looked after me like a little sister. He bought me my first pair of white Guess jeans for a school dance and taught me how to roller skate. They were always commenting on how cute I would be as a couple with Kamel's nephew, Ricky, but I wasn't interested. Kamel avoided any such talk around my aunt and uncle since I wasn't permitted to have boyfriends. But that never stopped Tori, who even set up a meeting that didn't work out.

One day, Tori and Kamel's relationship truly ended amid accusations of cheating. Tori cried all the time. We all grieved, sharing hopes of another reunion as they always did, but soon, Tori moved on to new suitors. She wasn't truly over Kamel, but she was desperately trying to be. With Kamel, we had all felt some reassurance that Tori was safe. Now, anything was possible.

I couldn't see Alex, but I talked to him at least three times a week for a few minutes at Grandma's. I needed something else to do to keep me busy once cheerleading was over—I had too much free time and was too young to work. I was planning our yearly youth church retreat but for the most part, everything was already done.

An ad inviting teenage girls to compete in the California Teen Pageant offered me an opportunity. I looked at the requirements— good academic performance, community service, and talent. I had the good grades, the service record, and I had talent. *Why not? It could be fun.* I completed my application and mailed it in.

Two weeks later, the letter came. "Congratulations . . ." I was invited. I showed Auntie and Uncle the letter.

"Wow, I didn't know you were even interested," Auntie said.

"I wanted to try something different. What do I do now?" I asked.

"I'm not sure, let's look at the rest of it," Auntie said. The packet included the rules, expectations, requirements, and competitions I would be involved in. A big part of it was fundraising for charity. In total, I had to raise money for a good cause, perform a talent or recite a speech, and show grace, beauty, and the confidence expected of a princess. But no one could tell me what to expect since no one else in our circle had ever done it.

"We were debutantes for our sorority, so we could help you some. It's kind of like that," Tori and Auntie offered, and described their experiences.

Auntie and Tori came up with the idea of making buttons with my picture on them as an advertisement to gain sponsors and support. As shy as I was, that would help a lot. At times, I had to be a salesman, but luckily, people were supportive, and a studio photographer offered to sponsor me in exchange for using my photos in her studio.

I raised a good amount of money, but it was clear that the sky was the limit in this competition. Before long, the three-day weekend event arrived. It was hectic, exciting, and scary. Adult pageant coordinators gave us instructions and helped us to get acclimated.

I was surrounded by tall, glamorous, confident girls—many familiar with each other from previous events. I was short, with a heavy accent, and it was my first time in a pageant, so I was intimidated. I even needed extra padding for my bra to fill in the missing space. I clearly had no idea what I was getting myself into, again. The girls dressed and undressed no matter who was around, complete with accessories, makeup, and bright smiles that appeared on cue, when just seconds before they were stressed or angry. I was usually hiding backstage trying to find a spot to get dressed, praying no one would see me, and makeup wasn't even in my vocabulary except for lip gloss.

We had lunches, practices, dinners, and inspirational sessions to increase our self-confidence as well as to give us pointers on how to handle the competition. Showtime was both scary and exhilarating—standing center stage before the judges and hundreds of people. As a group, we performed a song and dance number, and then one by one, each contestant paraded around, first in their bathing suit and later in their evening gown.

When it was time for the talent portion, I wished I had prepared a dance instead. I had an intelligent and heartfelt speech prepared about the importance of parents supporting their children, but once I was up there looking out into the crowd, I froze. I managed to say the first two lines but then went completely blank. My mind raced to some of the lessons we learned by the coaches . . . breathe, don't panic, focus, and keep going.

The audience was quiet.

"God, help me remember," I whispered.

I took a deep breath and continued with the rest of my speech, piecing it back together like a puzzle until it resembled what I had originally written. It was well appreciated by the crowd, and thankfully I made it through without fainting.

I imagined my mom in the audience. She would have been proud of me. Ronnie would have made fun of my flouncy white, swanlike dress.

What were they up to?

I didn't take home the big prize, but was honored to be considered amongst those talented, beautiful girls in such an elaborate, elegant, Cinderella-like gala.

Drama

A week before the school year was over, my friend Anita called to tell me about the drama club trip to New York. Of course, Alex was going and Antoinette, a popular girl who was also in the drama club and part of my cheerleading squad, now liked him. Anita thought that he liked her, too. Excruciating pain throbbed through my chest and my mind supposed all sorts of painful situations. I was at home and it was only 6 p.m., but I took a chance and called him once I was off the phone with Anita. He wasn't expected home until nine, which was after my curfew. My heart and stomach intertwined for the next three hours and I couldn't eat dinner. Right at nine I finagled the phone to my room, telling my aunt and uncle a fib about homework, and dialed. Alex picked up the phone.

"Hello?" he said.

I took a deep breath.

"Hi, it's me, are you busy?" I asked, my voice and body trembling.

"Yeah," he responded. Silence.

"I want to talk to you . . ." I started when I had enough courage. But before I could go on, there was a clicking sound—someone else had picked up the phone somewhere in the house.

"Hello?" Uncle said.

"Hello," Alex responded.

"Who's this?" Uncle David asked, his voice rising.

"Alex," he responded.

"Alex? Well, she can't talk to you. It's late."

"Okay. Bye." Alex hung up the phone.

So did I and waited for Uncle.

Within a minute he was in my room, face dark with anger. I was sitting on my bed, ready to cry. He walked up to me, slapped me hard across the face, grabbed the phone, told me I was grounded, and left the room. I was in shock from being hit, but also about Alex. The next few minutes were unbearable, but eventually I managed to go to sleep.

The next day was just as hard. It was hard to breathe, and my body was alert—on edge, experiencing a different type of fear. Despite my uncle's anger, I couldn't focus on anything but Alex. What was wrong with me? I prayed to God to help me. The day dragged by and three o'clock couldn't come fast enough for me, but when it did I was ready to dial at Grandma's house.

"What are you doing?" I asked, trying to control the tremble in my voice.

"Nothing. Are you okay?" Alex replied, referring to last night's incident.

"Yeah," I said softly. "Can you talk?"

"Yeah."

"So, you're going to New York with the drama club?"

"Yes."

"I heard something about you yesterday and I need to know if it's true," I said.

"What?"

I took a deep breath and tried to form the words.

"They say that you're going out with Antoinette. Is it true?"

He was quiet for moment, and then replied, "Yeah."

"Is that what you want? To be with her?" I asked.

"Yes," he answered.

"Are you sure?" I asked, hoping for a different answer.

"Yes. You can't even have a boyfriend," he said.

He was right of course, I wasn't supposed to have a boyfriend at all. Pain slowly filled my heart like liquid poison.

"Well, I guess that's it then. Take care of yourself," I said.

"Okay. Bye," he answered and hung up the phone.

I held the phone for a while, listening and hoping he was still on the other line. Moments later the dial tone jolted me to reality. It was over before it could begin.

My body started shaking although I was frozen in place. My mind went blank and panic crept through my body. Nauseous, I cowered on the bathroom floor. I let out a whimper, but quickly caught myself, knowing Grandma was on the other side of the door. I coached myself to breathe slowly in and out.

"Baby, you okay?" Grandma called out.

I composed myself. "Yeah, Grandma, almost done," I answered, trying hard not to let my voice betray me with a quiver.

My heart slowly tore, and I could barely breathe.

"Mom," I mumbled, trying not to sob.

Minutes later, I stood up, straightened my clothes, and joined Grandma in the living room trying to look normal. I sat down on the floor next to her chair, my heart aching and my chest ready to explode into screams, but I suppressed it. Grandma stroked my head tenderly, twirling the ends of my hair while watching *Murder She Wrote*. Her touch comforted me but also made me want to cry. I couldn't let her see my tears. I had to wait. This was my punishment.

"Please forgive me God," I whispered, holding back tears. "I'm sorry."

I read my Bible daily and prayed for guidance and strength.

"Are you all right, baby?" Grandma asked me, when a few days had passed.

As much as I needed her comfort, I had to suffer this heartache alone.

"I'm okay, Grandma," I responded, holding in my breath so that I wouldn't burst into tears. Somehow, comforting words had a way of always triggering my tears. When I was alone, the tears that flowed helped ease the pain cleansing my heart and soul, but shook my body uncontrollably. I longed for my mom and closed my eyes to imagine her holding me and caressing my hair. I needed relief.

I focused on Ronnie, thinking back to our adventures running around in the forest, climbing trees, and picking fruits and peanuts with friends.

Each night I read my Bible for encouragement, then turned on my landscape music and imagined Alex, Mom, Ronnie, and everything they meant to me. Eventually, I cried myself to sleep. For three months, it was my nightly routine—tossing, writhing and at times, balled into a fetal position praying to God, "Please help me. Please forgive me. Please let me forget. Please take care of Mom and Ronnie. Please," until sleep relieved me.

One night, I lay down on my bed, expecting to start sobbing quietly like all other nights, but I had no urge to cry. *I'm over it! I am free from torment.* Relieved, I prayed my thankfulness to God.

I was empowered, and fell asleep with a smile on my face, conjuring memories of Mom and Ronnie, hoping to spend time with them in my dreams.

Mom, Ronnie, I'm coming.

A few weeks after that, Alex called me at Grandma's house. I was unaware he even had the number. Luckily, I answered the phone, but hearing his voice didn't stun me—I didn't flinch, nor did my heart jump for joy. He asked why I didn't call him for his birthday and mentioned that he and Antoinette broke up. I reminded him we weren't together anymore. I didn't bother to address his new relationship status. I simply excused myself, saying I had chores to do, and hung up. Breathe. Feel. *Nothing.*

I was ready for the next part of my life.

Tenth Grade

M y excellent academic record and extracurricular activities brought the opportunity for me to apply and be accepted to a "magnet school"—Shadow Oaks Center for Enriched Studies—a specialized scholar program geared toward preparing students for college. It was about thirty miles away from home, but I could get there by bus. On my first day, Auntie dropped me off at the bus stop and I waited. I was intimidated, but I prayed to meet a friend. When the bus arrived, I stepped up to see if there were any takers and made eye contact with a pretty black girl with a stylish, shoulder-length hairstyle and the whitest, straightest teeth I had ever seen.

"Hi, my name is Destiny," she said, "You can sit with me."

"Hi, I'm Eliza, thanks," I replied, sitting down.

"Is this your first year at SOCES?" she asked.

"Yes. You?" I asked in return.

"No, I've been going there since I was in first grade. My brother goes there, too," she said, pointing at a handsome boy with curly hair. He reminded me of Alex, except taller and more muscular.

"Do you like it?" I asked.

"Yes, it's all right. It's better than the other high schools," she answered.

We went on and on, talking about our summer activities, our previous schools, and whatever else we could squeeze in between breaths in our forty-five-minute ride to school. It wasn't a big school, but only a select number of students could enter and return each year to keep the student-teacher ratio down and maintain the integrity of the program. The class size was low in comparison to other public schools and most of the children had started when they were in kindergarten. I was lucky to be selected to attend at this late stage, but their rules said if I ever chose to disenroll, I could not come back.

The school was well-kept and maintained. Beyond the gates were administrative offices and further down were hallways leading to classrooms, busy with students. To our disappointment, Destiny and I found that we would only have one class together, but we agreed that we'd have recess and lunchtime to catch up. Destiny was acquainted with most of the students, except for the few new students. *Going to the same school for eleven years, I wonder what that's like.* Destiny exchanged warm greetings and smiles, but kept me close. She introduced me to everyone—most were friendly, with only a few acting more standoffish.

The teachers seemed fair, but expectations were high. At lunch time, Destiny and her friend Vicky were at our designated spot. Vicky was tall, with braided hair and the sort of curvy hips many women would love to have. She was intelligent, quick, and funny. Vicky also took the bus to school, but she lived in Los Angeles, the opposite direction from us. The three of us were well matched in personality and had the same low-key demeanor. I thanked God for blessing me and wondered if Ronnie was in school, too. I spent most weekends with Destiny and thankfully Uncle and Auntie liked her.

"Grandma had a stroke and she's in a coma," Uncle explained.

What does coma mean? Grandma had been in and out of the hospital for years, but she always recovered.

"I know she's ready to go. She's always saying she feels like she's all alone and she's ready to go. She's the only one left from her family since she was the baby. But she has us, so I don't understand," Uncle said. "I know she's tired. She had a mastectomy from cancer, and she has high blood pressure and diabetes, and the doctor says the plaque buildup in her arteries is what has been causing the strokes. She can't stand taking all those medications. She calls them 'horse pills,'" he said, smiling slightly at the recollection.

I agreed. The pills were huge and she took so many different kinds. I remembered her telling me, "I'm ready to go. I'm tired. I don't wanna keep eating that ol' nasty food and I'm tired of going to the hospital. I don't like being a burden to anybody. They say I'm not, but I know I am. There's nothing left for me here. Your grandpa is gone, my sisters are gone, and I'm by myself." Her diet was bland, her body ailing. I stayed quiet and listened. *Was that her way of getting me ready for when she leaves me?*

We went to the hospital at every opportunity to spend time with Grandma even though she wasn't awake. I didn't like the hospital—it smelled like a lot of medications mixed with raw flesh—but I needed to see Grandma. I was sure she didn't like the smell either. She used to mention to me that she didn't like hospitals, maybe that was the reason. Uncle prayed over her and I watched, unsure of what to do. She had tubes through her nose and mouth, which scared me. *Can she hear us?*

When I couldn't go to the hospital, I stayed with Destiny so Uncle and Auntie could visit her. I prayed for her every day, but was unsure what to ask for since I knew she was ready to go, but I didn't want her to leave. I asked for her not to suffer.

Two months later, she passed away. It was devastating to all of us since she was our glue. The coma was her way of preparing us for what was to come. She was done with the prodding and needles poking her body. God listened to her. During her last years, she had friends who were trying to convert her to Jehovah's Witness. They didn't succeed, but she welcomed their visits and listened patiently. Maybe she managed to convince them.

"Where's Grandma's body?" I asked my uncle on our way home from the hospital.

"At the hospital," he answered.

"Are they going to bring her to our house?" I asked.

"No, baby, she's going to the mortuary, so they can prepare her for burial," he answered.

In the Philippines, the dead person's body would lie in the coffin at their own home as relatives, friends, and neighbors gathered day and night for about a week or so. The family would accept donations for the burial costs as well as say goodbye. Imagine being a child in that home with a dead body just down the stairs! Grandma's body was in a mortuary, but when I went to see her, she looked unreal. I got scared and walked away as soon as I could. Uncle and my father were grief-stricken—their only parent for so many years, Grandma had been a source of strength. Auntie arranged the funeral and arranged all the final plans, displaying her strength and allowing the brothers time to grieve. I didn't expect the ceremony to happen so quickly, but knowing what Grandma wanted helped me to accept that physically she was gone, but in spirit she would remain.

I hadn't seen my father and his family since moving back in with Uncle. They had not visited our home while Grandma was in a coma, my father went straight to the hospital a few times to see his mother, but it was difficult for him since she was unresponsive. Seeing Ms. Ama again turned my stomach into knots. Was there talk of me going back to them since Grandma was gone?

I prayed for mercy.

The extended time altogether highlighted the tension between Ms. Ama and Auntie Sheryl. They were two very different women. Ms. Ama was dependent and domestic and Auntie was independent and hardworking. They were both strong, but critical of each other. Ms. Ama complained that Auntie didn't take care of Uncle and Auntie claimed that Ms. Ama catered to my father excessively. Auntie was independent, but she believed in shared responsibilities. Ms. Ama, a devout Filipina Catholic, was raised to be submissive, with her top priority being taking care of her husband. They managed a cordial relationship during family events, but the wall between them was thick.

But once my aunt found out about the abuse against me, her dislike for Ms. Ama deepened. Auntie had endured physical abuse at the hands of her stepfather like I did and her mother failed to protect her child. After that, it was harder for Auntie to be around my father and Ms. Ama, opting to stay home when we went for visits, further alienating my aunt and Ms. Ama, who believed Auntie's place was next to Uncle.

Ms. Ama didn't like Tori either, after Tori spanked Jason for being in the pool despite warnings not to go in. How he ended up there was not clear, but Tori punished him since she was in charge. When the parents came back from their "adults only" evening out, Jason went sobbing to his mother with the story and she was infuriated. If it were me, I would have been brutalized, but she couldn't touch Tori, so instead she just muttered under her breath and glared. With Grandma gone, there was no need for her to keep up appearances.

Following the funeral, life returned to its routines, but the holidays proved to be difficult without Grandma. It wasn't the same without her smile, laugh, and calming presence. It was especially hard for the brothers, newly parentless while family unity was being celebrated. It was a sad and somber holiday season, full of reflection for the adults and mixed feelings for the children. Rather than celebrate the holidays together, each family unit did so separately.

As Destiny and I got to be closer friends, it wasn't long before she and her boyfriend Corey introduced me by three-way phone to Noe, Corey's best friend. Destiny had met Noe once and showed me a picture of him posing with Corey. He was cute. We talked on the phone whenever possible and found we had similar goals and temperaments. He played football, ran for his school track team, and was smart in school. Unfortunately, he lived in Los Angeles—which meant we couldn't see each other. Despite the distance, we agreed to go steady and our song was "Can You Stand the Rain" by New Edition—fitting since we had to endure. My sixteenth birthday was still two months away, so Uncle David wouldn't allow me to date officially, but allowed me to talk to Noe on the phone.

"Is he cute?" Tori asked me, smiling. I loved it when she was in a good mood.

"Yeah, I think so," I replied, showing her a picture.

"Oh, he is cute! Look at you!" she teased, elbowing me lightly with a huge grin.

Even though we lived in the same household, Tori and I operated under two very different sets of rules, governed by two very different people. Uncle was strict and protective, while Auntie Sheryl was fair and lenient—at times, Auntie and Tori acted more like friends than parent and child. I wished for my mom every time I saw them together.

I was still dubbed the "golden child" by auntie but she had to follow me in her car one day when I ran down the street, thinking I was going to get another spanking for forgetting to call her after school. Fortunately, this time around, Uncle wasn't going for it, but I don't actually know if Auntie even asked.

"Get ready, I'm gonna take you to see Noe for Valentine's Day! I already talked to him," Tori said. Her boyfriend was more than willing to help us; he would do anything for Tori.

"What? How? What about Uncle?" I asked.

"Don't worry, he won't care. I'll tell my mom. You're sixteen next month and I'll be with you. Plus, you have to see your Valentine!" she insisted.

Reluctant, but electrified, I got dressed, the sting of the last spanking still making me shiver. I slipped on the white jeans Kamel had given me and a blouse Tori helped me pick out. I was looking forward to seeing Noe in person, but I was also nervous.

After a long, nerve-wracking drive, I was pleasantly greeted when we arrived at Noe's cousin's home. Noe was tall, thin but muscular, with a light tan complexion, and he smelled great—Joop cologne, I would find out later. He was well dressed, had nicely trimmed hair, and wore braces that were small and clean. He looked as nervous as I did. We had good chemistry, but it was still awkward. He handed me a stuffed animal as a gift for the special day. Tori stood by the car, grinning from ear to ear and saying "Ooh" as if she was watching two little toddlers.

Tori and her boyfriend insisted on sitting at a different table when we went out for ice cream, so we could have privacy. Tori was still grinning and her boyfriend was having to vie for her attention. They had nothing to worry about with Noe; he was very much a gentleman.

By the end of our "date," we were comfortable with each other, but the awkwardness returned in anticipation of our first kiss, which turned my stomach topsy-turvy and shaky.

"Relax," he whispered. I took a deep breath and the shaking stopped. I closed my eyes, to experience the most passionate and electric touch on my lips. Foreign sensations ran through my body while I was as light as a feather. I understood his feelings without a word being said. I understood now why Uncle was leery of black boys.

A few more minutes passed in a blur; it was time to go and we embraced. Tori and her boyfriend were waiting in the car, and before we attracted any suspicion, I said I had better go. We hugged each other one last time and I walked away.

During our ride home, Tori bombarded me with questions about my experience. I couldn't stop smiling and answered her questions quite a bit embarrassed. I hoped Uncle wouldn't be home to see me with this big smile on my face. If he saw me, he would know, and I would be sure to get more than a slap. Luckily, he wasn't home.

Before bed, I kneeled and prayed, "Please forgive me for sneaking out. Thank you for keeping us safe." I snuggled in bed and recalled my night. *Would Mom be mad if she knew?* Ronnie would be protective. *Were they still living with Grandma under her house?* I imagined the tattered, moldy, and insect-ridden home. I hoped they had moved from there, but were still together. *Good night Mom, good night, Ronnie. Good night, Grandma.*

Now sixteen, I talked openly about Noe, but then Alex returned and stuck around, bold enough to come over and ask my uncle if he could visit me at home. Bold because Uncle had the reputation of being the tough and scary pastor when it came to his little women. Of course, Uncle remembered the "parking lot" incident with Alex. But, surprisingly, Uncle was impressed by Alex's honesty and respect and allowed him to come over as long as I agreed. Alex warmed Uncle's heart and sometimes they would sit and talk even when I wasn't home. On days I didn't have any plans, Alex offered to come over and teach me about Nintendo, showing me how to play games he had already mastered. Sometimes I would catch him staring at me intensely as if he had lost something. Noe didn't mind my having company. "I trust you, I know you wouldn't do anything," he said. "I have girl friends too, so I understand."

I continued to do well in school, earning As and Bs—if I got a C, it was in math. Cheerleading was out of the question since I didn't get to try out the previous semester (the school didn't have a football team, but we had a basketball team). I talked to the junior varsity drill team captain and told her my experience as a cheerleader and she gave me a try-out. She not only let me join the team, she asked me to be the co-captain since most of the team members had no prior experience. About a month later, our captain quit so she could focus on academics. She offered me her position since I had the most experience and I agreed, though I was somewhat apprehensive, since I didn't have any experience in this type of leadership.

My team needed a lot of help, but they worked hard, despite being embarrassed by the cheerleading and varsity drill squads who watched and giggled at our mishaps.

"It's okay, girls, we'll get it right," I assured them.

Surprisingly, the teasing fueled their spirits and we became stronger as a team. In our first performance, we made a couple of mistakes while lining up, but once the music started, we wowed the crowd, much to the dismay of the other squads.

At home, life changed for the worse. Uncle and Auntie were fighting every day and they weren't quiet about it, with doors slamming, stomping throughout the house, yelling and screaming. I tried to stay out of the way, but Tori sometimes joined in to help her mom, which escalated the arguments. The fights were about simple things like the use of the computer or typewriter, but that was just the surface. I didn't understand. *What changed?*

"Where is your golden child, we're gonna get her!" Auntie threatened in rage one fight night.

I cowered in my bed. *What? Me? What did I do?*

Soon after, Tori came in my room.

"Don't worry, we're just saying that to scare your uncle," she said. "We're not gonna hurt you. Go in your closet," she ordered and left.

I hurried in and tried to drown out the noise and chaos by covering my ears. It was worsening by the minute. "God, please make them stop," I prayed.

"You're not laying a hand on her!" Uncle yelled at Tori in the hallway. Sounds of stomping and a scream of agony followed. I didn't move, scared.

Tori started yelling, obviously enraged at Uncle. He must have hurt Auntie.

Soon after, thankfully, police officers were knocking at the front door. I was still hiding when they arrested Uncle and took him to jail. Scared, I stayed in my room and cried. Before long, Auntie came in and I saw what had caused her to scream. Her fingers were bent to the side. It was awful to look at, but at the same time I couldn't look away.

"I'm sorry if we scared you, we wouldn't hurt you. We know he cares about you, so it was the only thing we had on him," she confessed, obviously in pain. "I'm gonna go the hospital so they can snap my fingers back in place. I'll be back," she said.

She and Tori left for the hospital. I was in the house alone, in silence. Uncle spent the night in jail, but no charges were ever filed, since it was an accident.

"That was the most humiliating day of my life. I will never forgive her for that. She grabbed me tight by the shirt when I was trying to get to you and when I moved her fingers snapped. No one has ever done that to me. I can't trust her," he shared with me the next day.

I stayed quiet, not knowing what to say. I didn't understand why they fought. I didn't understand anything.

After that, I spent my weekends at Destiny's house. My uncle preferred that, especially while he was at work. He was worried about leaving me with Auntie and Tori, unsure if they would harm me. So much had changed in the past year, I never expected what was happening to happen. I had once asked Auntie if she believed she and Uncle would last forever.

"Yes, I believe we'll grow old together," she answered.

What happens now? Is this all my fault? Uncle was protecting me— who would protect him? Who will protect all of us?

God was in their hearts, so how did their hearts also house anger? They gave so much to others—not just the church, but by allowing people to live with us, or rent a room. They took in foster children and gave faithfully to the needs of others. When it came to each other, I guess they had nothing more to give. They were spent.

At home during the week, love, family, and home no longer existed; the tension and sorrow was thick and heavy. Conversations were slim to none—silence filled the home. Auntie and Uncle hardly spoke to each other and Tori stayed out as much as she could. A dark cloud was over us and I began to feel out of place again. They barely tolerated each other—the home that used to be a warm, safe haven was cold, strained, and quiet. The arguments and yelling stopped, yet it was clear that something was brewing. I wished for anything to release the deafening silence. I prayed for God's help.

Uncle was rarely home, choosing to work all the time with no days off plus overtime. Auntie worked and ran the home as usual, but was distant and moody. Tori was rarely home. I involved myself in extracurricular activities and began my first job. Destiny and I both got hired at Furr's Cafeteria, where we worked after school. On days he could pick me up, Uncle taught me how to drive in nearby empty lots, and at sixteen, I earned my driver's license. Mom would have been proud.

Life was full of activities and commitments between school, coaching, and work. I talked to Noe when I could, but the distance and inability to see each other strained our relationship. We had only seen each other in person twice. The second time, I met his mother—a kind, hard-working woman, committed to caring for foster children with physical disabilities. His brother in prison also reached out, writing a letter to me that expressed how much Noe cared about me; he also wrote about how lonely it was to be in prison and asked me to be pen pals if possible. Uncle had taught us our responsibilities to people in need as Christians, so I agreed, sharing the routine of my daily life and hopes for the future. He and Tori also became pen pals and at times I noticed wide smiles, exclamations, and blushing when she read his letters. I didn't want to know why.

In the attempt to reunite our family, Uncle and Auntie decided that we needed to be home more often and spending the night at other people's homes was forbidden. The tension remained, which made the weekends more difficult. My only reprieve was work, and I accepted every opportunity for more hours. Mondays couldn't seem to arrive soon enough so I could go back to school. I grew to hate weekends again, feeling anxious about a potential explosion, remembering Auntie's mangled fingers. I hoped to be anywhere else when it happened.

All the while, we went to church on Sundays and presented a united family. The moments others were around us, we shined.

The end of the school year was nearing and I was not looking forward to it. Prom was coming up, which was a welcome distraction. At our school, students were nominated for the royal positions of King and Queen for the seniors, Prince and Princess for the juniors, and Duke and Duchess for the sophomores. The air was filled with excitement and anticipation as to who would be nominated. The positive energy was a welcome change from the suffocation at home. During the nomination announcements, I was daydreaming about seeing my mom when I was awakened by a congratulatory hug from a friend sitting beside me in class. *Who in the world nominated me?* I was speechless, but managed to thank everyone once I was out of my stupor. Then I laid low, attempting to tone down the attention.

"I didn't do it," Destiny insisted, as she congratulated my nomination with a smile and a hug. The other nominees were varsity cheerleaders and all of them had attended the school since kindergarten. I was honored to be nominated, but didn't expect to win, since it was my first year.

The preparations for prom and the upcoming summer break spurred a variety of conversations about shopping with mothers and going on family trips or vacations, which made me feel envious. I wished I could talk to my mom, see her. I wished for her every day, imagining us shopping, eating lunch, or just sitting together laughing with Ronnie beside me.

Everything was upside down in life. I wished Auntie and Uncle were okay again. I wanted the fighting to stop. I focused on Mom, Ronnie, Grandma, God, everything good in my life. Noe, Destiny, school, drill team, prom—I had plenty to be grateful for.

Preparing for prom was exciting and distracting. With the money I earned from working, I bought a simple pink and white dress, with white shoes to match. That night, I was nervous and on edge since I was going on a date with Noe and nervous about the results of the nominations. At the event, everyone looked so pretty and I feasted my eyes on the variety of colorful dresses in different shapes and sizes. At a mere ninety-five pounds, with a skinny body and a flat chest, I was a little out of place next to my curvaceous peers.

The auditorium was elaborately decorated with balloons and sparkles, and there was a long table filled with refreshments. Some students were standing around talking or flirting, some were already dancing to the music, others were busy with last-minute preparations and the faculty was watching students to discourage bad behavior.

Noe and Corey met us at the front door of the auditorium and I was elated. Noe looked at me with pride, setting my cheeks flushing pink every time I caught his gaze.

Most of the evening was spent on mingling and dancing, until the moment of the announcement of the royal crowns. The King and Queen were as expected—the senior school sweethearts whose volatile relationship reminded me of Tori and Kamel. Next, the Prince and Princess were announced—no surprise there either, as cute and lovely as the first couple. I hung onto Noe, stiff as a doll, my heart pounding wildly in my chest. Sensing my tension, he held me closer.

"Don't worry, you're going to win," he whispered.

"And the winner is—Eliza Jackson . . ." For me, time stopped for a moment. Shocked, I looked around. Everyone was clapping and cheering as I was escorted to my seat for the coronation. It was unbelievable, incredible. I wished Mom and Ronnie could see me; Ms. Ama, too. Tears ran down my cheeks. For the rest of the night I floated on air as I danced with Noe. For the night, I was Cinderella.

After prom, Destiny's mom picked us up and let us stop at Beef Bowl to get food—we'd both been too excited to eat at prom. Destiny and I talked all night, laughing, giggling, and recalling all the special moments. The following day, I went home and shared my wonderful news with my family. Despite the turmoil in our home, they were joyful for me. But once the moment was over, we all went back to the gloom that seemed to have settled indefinitely. I replayed the night in my head, reliving my moment of pure happiness. I had won despite odds, which gave me hope of more to come.

I could hope. God was on my side.

The last few weeks of school were difficult since it had become, once again, my first place of escape. *Where will I hide now?* Fear set in, a familiar pattern that beset my life. Happiness followed by disappointment. I shook the worries from my mind and hoped for the best—grateful for my year of fortune.

I was chosen to spend a week at UCLA as an early introduction to college life. Fortunately, Destiny and Vicky were also invited, which made the trip more enjoyable. They tried to separate us into groups to mingle with others, but we always ended up back together like magnets. The week was an eye-opening experience and I looked forward to college life, thrilled about living in the dorms, on my own and independent. In two years, I could make my own decisions with no more worries about tension at home, and I could focus on my future. By the end of the trip, I was confident and looked forward to junior year. Still, my heart was heavy by the absence of my mom. How were she and Ronnie? Would I hear her voice again?

Summer Time

D uring summer break, my time was spent on preparing for our yearly church youth retreat in Riverside. My relationship with Noe suffered because of the distance; we couldn't talk as often and Uncle wouldn't let me be his date to go to his prom, so he had to go alone. Uncle preferred Alex, but also feared for my safety because of the ongoing gang wars and violence between the "Bloods" and the "Crips." The news was full of stories of members' grisly fates and those of innocent people caught in the crossfire during shootings. Fear and death jammed the news. Uncle was my protector, and I understood.

Noe and I talked sporadically, then less and less, until we stopped completely with no discussion. After a month of silence, I accepted it was over.

I still had no plans on rekindling anything romantic with Alex—as far as I was concerned, we were just friends, although he had grown on the rest of my family with his kindness and persistence. He even asked to join our church retreat, though he wasn't a member. Auntie and Uncle were impressed. I was unsure about the idea, still craving space to grieve over my breakup with Noe; nevertheless, he went.

When we arrived at our retreat site, right by the beach, the sun was just beginning to rise, and the weather was warm. We took a stroll along the water, staring in awe at the magnificence of the ocean—both magical and intimidating, it made me feel even smaller, yet special.

It was God's gift: "I made this for you and I created both of you."

The retreat was successful, with about a hundred or so young people attending. We sang, praised, and prayed together, and in our free hours, we frolicked on the beach. The water reminded of home—the Philippines—with Mom and Ronnie. I wondered if they were watching the same sun as it set. I closed my eyes and imagined them with me.

"God, please let me see them again," I whispered.

My focus in being at the retreat was to be of service and so I didn't pay much attention to Alex, who grew frustrated with my indifference and expressed it in revenge, embracing the attention of other girls. I noticed, but couldn't care less, which saddened him even more.

"Alex really loves you, can't you see that? He's been trying all year to make it up to you," Auntie Sheryl said.

"If you're not careful, you're going to lose him," Tori warned me.

I considered their advice carefully and went looking for Alex on the beach.

"Hi," I said. He looked at me, eyes filled with sadness and confusion.

"Hi," he said, with a shy smile.

Silence.

The revival of the energy that exuded between us was more powerful than words could relay. He looked relieved and smiled at me with adoration. Surprisingly, my spirit was lifted and I was able again—without fear—to look into the eyes I had avoided for so long.

For the remainder of the retreat, we were inseparable—taking time to walk or bike along the beach once we were free each day.

Back at home, he came over every day since school was over and sometimes Destiny and her new beau, Alex's best friend, joined us. Once, I cooked Alex dinner—peppered steak, rice, and corn, and cake for dessert, which he enjoyed.

His family liked me as well, sometimes joining us when my father and his family visited. To everyone, it was clear we were meant to be together. I looked forward to a new life with him, imagining all the things we would do together.

Then, one day, my uncle said I was moving back to my father's house.

"Why, Uncle?" I asked, pleading.

"With everything that's going on here, your father wants you home. It's not a good environment for young ladies. He doesn't like you being in the middle of it and wants you home. I can't blame him, I want you safe, too," he answered sadly.

I understood, but it meant losing everything I had worked so hard for—school, Destiny, activities, and now Alex. Alex and Destiny were just as crushed and in disbelief, but all of us were helpless.

For the next few weeks, I spent every waking moment with Alex, and sometimes Destiny joined us. Uncle saw how close we three were and encouraged our time together. I recalled our beginning, getting grounded and smacked in the face for talking; how things had changed.

Goodbyes with Auntie and Tori were quick, subdued with hugs and well wishes.

"Please, God, help my family," I prayed, a little scared by thoughts of what could happen.

With all my bags packed in the trunk of Uncle's hatchback sedan, Destiny, Alex, and I piled in the back seat, me between my two best friends. We were a pathetic sight—all three of us with tears running down our faces. I glanced at Uncle and saw tears in his eyes, too.

When we arrived, Uncle and Destiny gave Alex and me alone time together. We promised to stay together regardless of our distance, but it was small comfort. Tender and tearful, we held each other close, hoping that by some miracle we didn't have to let go. But reality came swiftly. Uncle piled my things into my father's car and when he was done, hugged me goodbye.

"It's gonna be all right, baby," he whispered, kissing my forehead.

I've heard those words before, why I would believe them now?

I cried softly in his arms until it was time to go. Moments later, I was in the passenger side of my father's car.

As we drove off, I was overwhelmed by heartache. I stared at the side mirrors to catch last glimpses of the faces of those who loved me.

When will I feel that love again?

I didn't have the voice to scream. I hung onto the promise I had made with Alex and prayed silently for a miracle to survive what was to come ahead. *What did Ms. Ama have planned for me?*

Eleventh Grade Year

When we arrived in Las Vegas, I could see the little precious ones celebrating through the window. It was comforting. They rushed out and helped carry my things. I looked around the neighborhood . . . nice and clean with at least one large tree in front of each home.

"Thank you, God, that at least they love me," I whispered, as I watched the little beauties fuss about me.

Lacey had grown quite a bit, and was as cute as she could be, with thin straight hair that just hit her shoulders. She followed everyone around in all the excitement as if trying to figure out her part in the chaos. Jay was adorable, too, with his "bright eyes" (as Grandma called them) and straight, black hair like his sister. He was the most behaved of all the little ones, often the first to take a nap when I was in charge, especially when the prize was a pack of M&M's. Jason's smile was as big as ever, his hair just as curly, his mind probably brewing up something mischievous—for some reason, the thought made me smile. Candace had grown a bit, with long waves of hair spiraling down her back.

Ms. Ama sat in the living room, unmoved, during all the commotion, but managed to say hello when she saw me. I responded respectfully until I was rushed off into my room by my entourage. My room was nicely furnished with a new bedroom set which still had the new smell and didn't look cheap. Mine was the first bedroom and the rest of the bedrooms followed down the hallway in the single-story home. I began unpacking my things, beginning with my radio, as the little ones gathered around in amazement.

"What songs do you have?" Candace asked, trying to look in my bag. The rest of the crew looked on with curiosity, with the same adorable expressions that lifted my spirit.

"You wanna see?" I asked. They all nodded their heads in unison like a set of twins. I smiled and plugged in my cassette player, put in a tape, and pushed play. The party started as they began jumping up and down, singing along and dancing. It was my welcome home party. Otherwise I would be rolled up in a ball. Our father looked in and stood by the doorway enjoying the scene. Maybe that's what made him keep trying, these kids.

"Time to go to bed," Ms. Ama bellowed. The fun was over. I turned off the music and the disappointed entertainers left, leaving me alone to recover. Once the children were in bed, my father and Ms. Ama came to my room. He reassured me that I would not be mistreated. Ms. Ama stood quietly. He knew.

For the first two months, nothing bad happened. But by the third month, the mutterings began, accompanied by piercing looks. The familiar tension grew until it was as thick as mud. I already had an escape plan and made myself scarce as much as possible. When I came home at night following my after-school activities, food was hidden so that I couldn't eat. I had been hungry before; I survived.

School was quite a distance away from home, which meant I had to depend on my father. I prayed he wouldn't let me down.

Luckily, Lindley also attended the same school, which allowed us to reconnect as though I never left. Her spunky spirit reminded me to fight for my survival.

"Is your stepmother still mean?" she asked, scowling.

I nodded.

"Ugh," she said. "What's her problem? You're such a good kid. My mom always asks me why I can't be more like you and get good grades," she laughed, tapping my arm lightly.

"You have so many talents, you're perfect just as you are," I answered.

"Yeah, you're right, I do," she said, her eyes lighting up as she began singing and dancing—two things Filipinos love to do. God blessed her with a lovely voice and I was blessed to be the one to enjoy it. Since she was in the choir, she convinced me to take the class as an elective.

"Sometimes we go out of town on competitions and we practice after class," she offered, winking.

I had never considered singing, but practice every day and a class we two friends could share, sold me.

Our school choir was nationally recognized and competed every year nationwide. I also signed up for honors to improve my transcripts, but unfortunately, it was too late for me to try out for cheerleading. I decided this was my last move; no more moving back and forth. Spend two years in the same school—that was my goal.

For the next couple of months, I busied myself with schoolwork and choir. Lindley brought me up to speed on her life while I was gone since talking long distance on the phone meant a large phone bill our parents would have been unwilling to pay.

On rare occasions, I went to her house to hang out. Her room was like Tori's, so much stuff, not enough space, although it was cleaner and organized. Sitting on her bed, we talked and played music while she sang along. She and Lenny got together for a few months, but eventually they broke up and he went back to his ex-girlfriend.

"He still calls me sometimes to hook up." She smiled mischievously, but got quiet after studying my face.

"Do you go?" I asked.

"Yes, I know I shouldn't, but I love him," she explained, moaning.

I shook my head and rolled my eyes. When I turned back to look, her eyes stared in the distance with a sweet smile on her face.

"Oh, goodness!" I said, as she burst into laughter. She was so dramatic, a definite performer.

"But this other guy, John, likes me too. He's cute! We're supposed to go on a date," she said, swishing her sweet-smelling hair and going into her closet to find something to wear like a stage actress getting ready to dress for an act.

She asked me about Alex, and I told her, but it was painful. She understood and comforted me as much as she could. I preferred talking about her life that was livelier and less depressing. "Well, at least you're back here with me," Lindley said, smiling.

"Yeah, you're right," I said. It could be worse.

Alex . . . I couldn't talk to him as much as I would have liked — only when my father was home and encouraged me to talk for a few minutes.

I wished it was as easy to talk to Mom and Ronnie. I missed Alex, but Mom and Ronnie were my first and deepest loves. I prayed for them every night hoping they stayed safe until I saw them again.

Signing up for choir was a great decision — a new experience, a different talent. I loved the precision, discipline, and strength it took to sing together in perfect unison. Our teacher was of average height, a small-framed woman, but with a presence that exuded grace, strength, and command. I tried out and was chosen for the upcoming national competition in California as part of the second soprano section. Our choir had won the last three years of competition and we aimed to honor our teacher again.

On the day of the competition, we traveled very early by bus to the venue. We gasped as we entered the awe-inspiring auditorium. It was breathtaking, with rows and rows of seating for the invited audience. I was nervous, since hundreds if not thousands of people would be watching, but we were under a great commander. Lindley, by comparison, was ready to perform, only slightly nervous.

We performed the song "Danny Boy" and all I could hear was the harmony, precision, and passionate sounds we made together which sent chills up my spine. The audience was in an uproar once we finished, giving us a standing ovation; the judges agreed, awarding us first place. It was exhilarating to win for a teacher who'd taught us the strength of teamwork and discipline. It wasn't about winning a trophy or title; it was about reproducing the beauty of the music and performing well in honor of the artist.

I continued to do well in school with advanced placement classes and got involved in student government and social clubs. Naturally, they were good reasons to stay after school, so my father encouraged them.

Lindley and I were together most of our free time at school, but I also became friends with Natalie, a quiet, kind girl whose family came from Belize. We shared two classes together, and though she rarely spoke to others, we connected immediately and became more like sisters. I also became friends with Tawny, an attractive mixed-raced (Korean and black) girl, with creamy mocha-colored skin. Aside from her skin color and textured hair, her features were purely Asian. To correct her vision, she wore stylish, sixties-style glasses that accented her eyes even more. I appreciated Tawny's directness, individuality, and stubbornness—she didn't care what other people thought about her. I admired her strength. We shared many things in common including missing a parent. I didn't have my mother, she didn't have her father.

Second semester, I joined the track team. It was then Ms. Ama started complaining to my father that I was never home. *Why did she want me to come home, when she didn't want me to be at home?* My father knew I had joined the track team and encouraged it. The moments I was home, Ms. Ama merely glared at me, muttering something in Kapampangan. It couldn't be nice, so I ignored it. I had to keep moving, keep working, keep doing well in school, since it was my only chance to get out. I focused on the things I could control and as to the rest, I prayed to God for help.

For some reason, at five-foot-two and ninety-five pounds, I chose to run the hurdles, which were almost as tall as me. I stuck it out, since I liked challenges and my coach agreed, probably because there weren't many volunteers for the event. Our practices were gut-wrenching and tedious, especially for a newbie like me, with plenty of long and short runs for conditioning. There were times I was sure I was dying, since I couldn't catch my breath, felt light-headed, and even tasted what seemed like blood from my lungs. But after some time, my body adjusted to the new regime.

I did well at our first track meet, only because I didn't knock over the hurdles and I didn't come in last. I was proud of having accomplished that much and started to enjoy it. But a month after joining the team, tryouts for cheerleading began for the next season. I enjoyed track, but cheerleading was my passion and helped me forget everything. There were only a few openings and for most of the girls it was worth a try. I signed up with Lindley and Tawny. Natalie was too shy and giggled at the mere idea.

After school, the school gymnasium filled up with girls, even those already in the squad. Everyone had to try out each year to keep it fair and even, except for the captain and co-captain, who were chosen by the coaches. It was anybody's chance to win, and most were ready for the challenge. Every time the music started, or the commands rang out, for some, the movement was natural. It was thrilling to experience as well as to watch. But for others, it required greater effort to balance and merge the movements with the music and make it look fun. It was hard work for everyone.

"I don't want to be like them!" Tawny would often say disgustedly. "They think they're better than everybody, but we won't be like that," she added. She didn't care much about the current cheer team.

It was the opportunity to dance that brought us to tryouts— and for me, the added opportunity to stay away from home even more. I had the feeling that Tawny was running away from something, too, but from what? She shared that her mother was ill, and they had no other family members to help with her care. Being the only caregiver made Tawny a stronger, more mature teen.

As the week-long tryout continued, people began to dwindle away; they either quit or were eliminated. It was nerve-wracking and difficult, and in the end, only twelve girls remained on the squad, including Tawny and me. Unfortunately, Lindley was eliminated in the second round, but she was rooting for us.

Following the tryouts, the real work began as we learned new routines for summer camp, where we would join other squads from across the nation. Summer days in Las Vegas were at times ruthless, with no relief, but we were blessed to have the auditorium for practice. I was already busy, but I needed a job to pay for my cheerleading fees and extra activities like prom. Fortunately, I got a job at Carl's Jr. and worked about four hours a day after practice and got a ride from friends or my father to get home.

A few days a week, I also had practice for our school's yearly fashion show or attended meetings for school government or clubs. Tired, but motivated, I studied at night, during recess, and any breaks throughout the day, leaving myself no time to think about my problems. I didn't have time to daydream and join Mom and Ronnie, and at night I was too tired, although I always prayed for them every night after reading my Bible.

When I was at home, the kiddies would come in my room and listen to my stories. I told them about everything I did—cheerleading, school, clubs, anything and everything that was happening. Then music was requested so we could all dance and I could show them my routines. They were so innocent and easy to please. Sometimes I took them for a drive in the neighborhood in my father's two-door, broken-down, 1977 Buick Regal.

"This is going to be yours once I fix it," he said proudly.

Unfortunately, he never got around to it. The engine worked fine, but the interior seats were badly torn, and every time I turned a corner the passenger door swung wide open. That never stopped the kiddies from begging and piling in for a ride. It made the ride more exciting. Every time we approached a corner to turn, I slowed to a crawl, and they braced themselves and clung onto the door as tightly as possible. In the event of an unsuccessful hold, they just grabbed it and closed it as soon as they could, laughing at the top of their lungs. It was hilarious and unforgettable.

Still, they were impressionable. Every night, Ms. Ama assigned Candace the task of ensuring that I didn't go in the kitchen to eat. She would make sure that whatever she cooked was put away and hidden so that I couldn't find it without making some noise. Candace, who was twelve, obeyed, but it hurt her too. "She told me to make sure you didn't go in the fridge to get food to eat. I'm sorry," she confessed. "It's okay." I assured her. *I hate that she is put in this position, I just won't eat. The food didn't matter, I could eat at work.* Ms. Ama and I barely spoke a word to each other, but the tension was building thicker by the day. When Ms. Ama noticed I didn't eat at home, she complained to my father that I was eating too much fast food. I was confused.

I was starting to feel defeated. I missed Mom's laughs, hugs, and smile. I missed Ronnie and his protection. I missed Grandma teasing my hair. I missed Uncle's encouraging words. I missed Auntie's generous spirit. I even missed Tori's stories. I worked hard to build myself up, yet my path seemed pre-determined. I prayed, but everything remained the same.

Alex and I had managed to stay in contact, although irregular. By this time, my father was beginning to admit that things at home had unraveled again and seemed to struggle with what he could do to help me.

He often mentioned that he hated that he took me away from Alex. So did I, but I couldn't focus on that now.

"I'm glad you will get to see him soon," he added. Yes, prom night.

I was electrified to see Alex again, especially for prom—a promising night for rekindling romance. It had been nearly a year since we'd seen each other, but we hung on to our promise. He looked even more handsome, tall and muscular. It was wonderful to see my best friend again, holding each other in a long embrace before it was time to go to the dance. When we walked into the party and I introduced him to my friends, they were impressed. I had talked about him all the time and they finally got to see who I had been raving about. They finally understood, disproving their teasing theories of a phantom boyfriend.

It was a magical evening of dancing, glamour, and reconnection. At the end of the night, I was sad to see him go and he looked just as miserable. I looked at him—there was something he was dying to say, but wouldn't.

"Is everything okay?" I asked.

"Yeah . . ." he answered slowly.

We talked about the things that were going on in our lives and I told him my plans.

"I want to stay here and finish high school. I don't want to move again."

He looked at me, sad and confused about my decision.

"Don't you want to come home?" he asked.

"I do, but I'm tired of moving."

He tried hard to be supportive, but there was sadness in his eyes. We tried to shake off the sadness that was settling on us, realizing we only had a few moments left. After a kiss and hug, he had to go—our rides were waiting. I could only wish we had another day to spend together, but I had to settle for what I could get. Our day ended as fast as the year had passed. In a flash, he was gone again, and my heart went with him and I kept his. Still, I wondered what had weighed so heavily on his mind.

"What happened, what happened?" Candace asked, jumping up and down while the others looked on. My father stood by my doorway, looking just as interested.

"It was fun, we had a great time," I answered with a hint of sorrow.

"I'm sorry, baby; I wish you guys could be together," my father confessed. I didn't answer, just listened.

I shared a little more about my evening and noticed Ms. Ama turning on the washing machine and stuffing things in for a wash. The laundry area was right across from my room and I could see her opening and closing doors and muttering under her breath. I grew uncomfortable and distracted by the noise, so I cut my story short so the noise would stop. "And that's all . . ." I said, ending my story hoping my audience was satisfied.

"Well, when are you gonna see him again?" Candace asked, curious about Alex.

"I don't know," I answered sadly.

"Well, maybe we can take a trip over there for a visit," my father suggested, trying to lighten the mood.

"That would be nice," I responded, but it was a long shot. The dryer door slammed.

By this time, everything had escalated to the point that Ms. Ama tried to prevent me from going to school. I surmised she didn't like my alone time with my father. One day, I came home from school to find my alarm clock plug was bent. I reshaped it and plugged it back in. The following day, my alarm clock and lamp plugs were both bent. I reshaped them and plugged them back in. The next day or so, the iron was gone. I bought my own. Next day, that was bent too. Every morning or at night when I came home, I would find my things . . . whatever had a plug . . . all bent, and I reshaped them the best I could for the next day. I prayed they would hold up and not become irreparable with the constant bending and straightening. There were a couple of close calls when my alarm clock didn't work, and I barely made it to ride to school with my father, but I made it. Thankfully, my room was close to the kitchen so when he was in there eating breakfast I could hear him—that was my second alarm.

Through the years, there were times I hoped my father would acknowledge what was going on, but the time never came. It didn't matter. It was a moot point. I needed to survive and have a life of my own, but I could feel her anger brewing deeper and tenser every day. In time, she stopped muttering under her breath and said what was on her mind, even when my father was home. He probably hoped like I did that it would go away, and granted my every request to be away from home, which infuriated her even more. I was on borrowed time, and prayed for God to save me and give me strength for whatever was to come.

One afternoon, I came home to get clothes for cheerleading practice before work. I was packing a bag when Ms. Ama stood at my doorway.

"What are you doing?" she asked coldly, arms folded on her chest.

"I'm getting some things for practice. Then I'm going to work," I answered.

"No, you're not. You're never home and you cannot do this anymore. I am going to tell your father—you're not going anywhere!" she said, her voice elevating.

"Dad already knows," I responded.

"I don't care, you're not going anywhere!" she insisted, her pitch rising higher.

"I have to go," I answered, quite calmly, to my surprise. Ms. Ama was just as surprised.

"If you leave, then don't come back!" she said.

"Okay," I answered, which brought the shock level even higher for both us. I couldn't believe what I was saying, but I was overcome with a surge of power. It was true, I didn't care. I began packing all my things, though I had nowhere to go. Friends? I could ask Lindley, Tawny, or Natalie.

"What are you doing?" she repeated, getting angrier by the second.

I didn't stop.

She rushed toward me with her hand raised about to strike. Luckily, I turned in time to face her and grabbed the hand before it struck me. I held it. I had the arm, this arm that had tormented me for so many years—strong, white, and warm. It was an ordinary arm, no different from mine except in color of skin and painted nails. We stood face to face for moments that seemed like hours, both in shock in different ways.

I looked into her widened eyes. "You're *not* going to hit me again," I said simply.

Her face turned from anger, to confusion, to panic, within seconds, all the while she remained speechless. She pulled her hand from my grip and stepped back toward the door. Empowered, I turned back to finish packing, with no fear that she would try to hit me again.

"Where are you going to go? You can't leave!" she screamed, running in and out of my room. By now, the kiddies were gathering by the doorway, scared by their mother's yelling and my packing. I couldn't stay. Nothing would ever change. I was a guest who had overstayed her welcome. At least there would be peace without me. I didn't like the precious ones scared, tears forming in their pretty little eyes.

My father came home soon after to find Ms. Ama screaming, ranting and raving about what happened, some words unintelligible, especially with her accent. When he finally came into my room, I was sitting on my bed, bags packed. He sat next to me, both of us silent.

"I'm sorry about this," he said. "I'm sorry for taking you away from your uncle and from Alex. I wish I could change things. I thought it was going to be different this time . . . that she would change. I'm sorry you had to go through this again. I just really don't know what to do and I have the other kids to think about. I just can't stop her from doing these things. I'm so sorry, baby. I don't know what else to say."

I was relieved. I was alone, but I had the grace of God to see me through. Interesting enough, Ms. Ama never touched my Bible.

"So, where are you going to go?" he asked.

"I don't know," I answered, "I'll ask my friends."

"Let me know where you are when you get there," he added.

"Okay," I said, picking up bags upon bags. I took everything so I didn't have to come back.

I walked out of the house, struggling with my bags, wishing my father had offered me a ride. I didn't have a car and nowhere to put all the things I was lugging, and I sure couldn't take them to practice! I walked to a neighbor's house two blocks away. I'd said hello now and then to the teen that lived there since we went to the same school, but we were strangers. I was desperate, so I knocked. The mother answered, the teen behind her, peeking over her shoulder.

"Hi . . . Ummm, I was wondering, can I leave my things with you until I can get a ride to come back and pick them up?" I asked, hoping for relief.

"Of course, you can put them in the garage. Do you need a ride?" she asked. Up to that point, I had held my emotions together, but her heartfelt kindness brought me to tears as I accepted her generosity.

"Are you okay?" she asked, concerned.

"Yes, thank you for helping me," I assured her, nodding and wiping my tears.

I was seventeen years old, homeless, with no transportation, no money, and no family. I wished I could go home to my mom and Ronnie, but still no word from them. *I hope they're okay.* I was sure they didn't know how to find me just like I didn't know how to reach them. I had faith it was all going to work out. I was on my own, but God was with me.

Homeless

I got to practice on time, went to work, and met with Natalie after my shift. I told her what was going on.

"You can stay with me," she offered, smiling. "My family is going to Belize for the summer and I don't want to go. I'm sure they'll be more comfortable with me staying if I had a friend with me, so I won't be alone. Why don't you come spend the night and I can ask my mom in the morning?"

"Oh, thank you," I answered, thankful for the possibility.

The following morning, Natalie talked to her parents, who agreed to let me stay. They warned us to be safe and of course, they insisted: no parties. Natalie agreed and they trusted her.

"My aunt lives close by in case we need anything," she said after telling me the good news. "But really, we're on our own!" she added.

School was over, and we agreed it would be best for us to work together at Taco Bell, hopefully with the same schedule. They hired me on the spot and the following week, I started. I still had cheerleading practice three to four hours every day, and thankfully, Tawny gave me a ride to work. After work, Natalie and I grabbed two soft tacos each for thirty-nine cents each, walked home about two miles, smelling like ground beef, and ate once we sat down. We were glad for the convenience since most days we were too tired to cook—plus, we tried to limit how often we cooked for fear of burning down the house.

Summer days were hot, and nights were only a little cooler. Sometimes there were breezes; however, there were times we preferred no breeze since it was like hot air balloons blowing. Once home, between the heat and work, depleted from standing on our feet for hours, we barely had enough energy to wash our face, brush our teeth, and change for bed.

I was glad to be away from home, but I called my father to tell him I was safe. He asked I call occasionally to let him know I was safe. I did, but when Ms. Ama started answering I stopped calling. It was best to leave that life behind. I prayed I could stay with Natalie for the next year, thankful to God for the mercy of others.

Except for a small amount of pocket money, my earnings were spent toward my uniform, school supplies, and camp fees for cheerleading.

When the day came to leave for cheerleading camp, all bags packed, Tawny and I piled onto the bus headed to California. The drive took a few hours, and we arrived cramped and groggy, but still pumped up. There were about thirty other squads between the neighboring states—Nevada, California, Utah, and Arizona—all eager to perform. It wasn't a competitive event, but each squad performed for practice, feedback, to learn, and headed home looking forward to refining old routines and creating new ones.

After prom, Alex and I had grown further apart for more reasons than just distance. When we had the chance to talk, I told him about what was going on with me while he expressed his deep regret.

"Well, where are you going to live?"

"I don't know."

"Are you coming back home then?"

"I really don't want to. I still don't want to move."

Silence. He didn't say so, but that hurt him since this was an opportunity to be together again. I was over being a yo-yo and no matter where I lived, there were problems. I was being unfair, I knew, keeping him when he could have a relationship with someone close to him. Our silence over the phone expressed a thousand words neither one of us could say. It was time to move on and pass the torch, even though we still loved each other. Once we hung up the phone, I knew it was over.

Although disappointed, I had to be content with my life. I was determined to stay in Las Vegas, but reality was whispering in my ear. I dreamed a little longer.

"Hi, Uncle!" I said, upbeat and cheerful when I heard him on the line. I had delayed this conversation for too long.

"Hi baby! Where are you?" he asked, his voice filled with concern.

"I'm staying with my friend Natalie. She's really nice."

"Well, tell me where she lives so I can pick you up," he said.

"Uncle, I want to stay here. I don't want to change schools again. I can ask my friends if I could stay with them. Dad let me," I answered.

"No, baby, you can't stay out there. You need to come home," he said.

Home? Where is that?

"But Uncle, I got into cheerleading, I'm doing really good here. I just don't want to change schools again," I said.

"I know, baby . . . but you have to come home. I can't believe my brother let you be on your own out there like that. You're homeless. He should have told me so I could pick you up. I talked to him. He said he was sorry about taking you back from me. I'm sorry that I let you go back, but you can't stay out there."

I knew he was right. I couldn't go on being homeless in Las Vegas, staying with Natalie was only temporary. He would be here by week's end. I told Natalie what was to come. She and others offered to ask their parents, but I knew Uncle would never agree. I quit my cheerleading, my job, said goodbye to my friends and mentally prepared to leave Las Vegas.

As expected, Uncle was in front of Natalie's house on Saturday. I didn't recognize him at first since he'd lost so much weight. When I heard, "Hey, baby!" my spirits immediately lifted. I hugged him as soon as I could reach him. He meant home for me, just like Mom and Ronnie. I could breathe and let go of the fight. I looked forward to going back to California. I didn't look back. It hurt too much to do so.

"I had to really work on my weight, baby, it wasn't good for me. I went on a program and I ride my bike every day for at least two hours a day, rain, sleet or snow," he said, chuckling. It was wonderful to hear him laugh, and it momentarily reminded me of my mom's laughter. When he wasn't riding his bike, he was at work, so he was never home. He was running away from home, too, we had that in common.

"It hasn't been good, baby. I missed you. It's been tough. I didn't have anybody on my side," he teased. His relationship with Auntie had become more strained and they hardly spoke to one another. "Tori's never home either, but that's nothing different. I don't even say anything anymore, I gave up trying," he explained.

It was sad to hear, especially since they were two loving and kind people. *Why couldn't that love extend to each other? How does that happen?*

When I stepped into the house, it was just as I had left it—cold, distant, estranged, and lonely. People lived here with no love or warmth. I prayed for happiness for all of us. Next, I needed an escape plan. We were dodging bullets that nearly grazed us.

What will happen next?

Senior Year

F riends and neighbors welcomed me back and in no time, everything was in full swing as if I never left. I hadn't seen Chloe, but it wasn't long before she came knocking.

"I go to Fitzgerald High School now and I'm part of the Dance Production. I'm the co-captain," Chloe said, beaming.

"What about cheerleading?" I asked.

"I tried out, but I didn't make it. That's okay because we get to perform during halftime and we have a good team. Someone might be leaving, and we may need another person, maybe you can join us," she offered.

"Oh, that's nice. But I can't go to Fitzgerald since we're zoned for another school," I said, disappointed.

"That's okay, maybe the people letting me use their address can help you, too. I can ask," she offered.

"That would be nice. I really don't want to go that school," I added, referring to the nearby high school.

"No one does, ugh!" she said, making us both laugh.

I asked my uncle about the possibility of going to Fitzgerald and he said he would consider it since he had friends who lived nearby. Tori attended our local high school, and Uncle wasn't impressed. Uncle's friend gladly agreed to allow the use of his address and I was in. Plus, Chloe asked me to join their squad, since a member had indeed quit. Things were coming together brightly, which allowed me to let go of Las Vegas.

Summer flew by and we were back in school. I knew quite a few other students from cheerleading years ago and some lived close to me—many from Feldman. I started spending a lot of time in the administrative office and became close to the counseling and administrative staff, including Mrs. Hall, a counselor, and the principal's secretary, Mrs. Lith. Gossiping or checking out the guys didn't interest me, and I spent my free time looking for scholarships and getting ready for my final getaway plan—college. The administrators enjoyed seeing my enthusiasm and helped me even when I didn't ask.

Two months after I started school, the guilt from lying to get in the school became too much to bear. It reminded me of our ninth-grade conspiracy and how I felt when I was called into the office. I ended up confessing to Mrs. Lith, regardless of the consequence.

Mrs. Lith just smiled as if she had a secret. "Girl, don't worry about it," she said, waving her hand and laughing. "You're not the only one. We got all kinds of students here, some all the way from LA, but they get bused here, so don't worry. But it's good that you don't like to lie." She turned to face her computer still chuckling. "What is your address?" she said. I breathed a sigh of relief. *I don't have to leave after all and I can stop worrying.*

I told Uncle later about what happened. He held his breath on some parts, but relaxed when I told him the results. He was proud of my determination to be honest, even at a great risk of getting kicked out. I was overjoyed it worked out and thanked God in prayer before sleep.

Since I had moved around from so many different schools, it was a tedious task to make sure I completed all the required classes to graduate. I was a little scared because requirements between states were different, but thankfully, everything was in order when I met with the counselor. My focus became preparing for

SATs and/or ACTs and, of course, doing well. It was a stressful time for seniors—most hoping to get a high enough score to be accepted and waiting for replies.

I considered Pepperdine and Spelman but ultimately set my heart to attend the University of Irvine for their medical program. I must keep my promise, become a doctor, and help my mom. I was accepted to start at Irvine in the fall.

Uncle and Auntie were prepared to help me financially, but I applied for scholarships and grants to cover as much expenses as possible. I fantasized about living on campus and going to classes. Mom would be proud. Ronnie would join me.

"So, why didn't you call me when you got back?" Alex asked, standing in my doorway, looking upset.

"I didn't know what to say," I answered. I didn't say it, but I was focused on surviving and graduating; I had no time for distractions. Home was quiet; we all pretended. My goal was to relieve everyone from the burden of having to take care of me, like Grandma, and run toward a better life and right now that was college. Once I was gone, I'd always be independent. I could live on my own, make my own decisions, live without turmoil . . . live happily ever after.

Alex and I talked for a while, and went on a double date with Destiny and her boyfriend, but when it became clear his interests included sex, I couldn't move forward. We never went past holding hands and kissing, but since he'd had some sexual experiences with others, it was now his desire with me. I wasn't ready, and I didn't like the ultimatum. I was committed to waiting until marriage or at least until I was engaged. Though I understood his desire, I didn't like the pressure and wasn't ready for that kind of commitment. He figured out my answer when I didn't return his calls for days. He didn't like my inaction, and I would pay dearly for it.

I got a job at a shoe store at the mall with Destiny so I wouldn't have to ask Uncle and Auntie for money. They had enough to worry about and I was also saving up for a car. In the meantime, one of them still picked me up after my shift at 9 p.m.

One evening, while trying to arrange and rearrange shoes to look busy on a slow sales day, I looked up at the worst time to see Alex walking hand in hand with another girl—kissing him as they paraded past my store. My jaw dropped, I couldn't move. He looked at me, but he didn't look smug or delighted. Once my feet came unglued, I ran to the back of the store. I was trembling, mouth open, but there was no sound. Then, groans from deep within welled up from my stomach. My heart dropped to my stomach but got rejected back up. I was doubled over like someone had just kicked my stomach. I felt nauseous, and everything was spinning. I gasped for air like a fish out of water. Destiny was by my side to calm me down. She held me, rubbed my back, caressed my hair, and whispered, "It's okay. It's okay." Her kindness and understanding were enough to get me through the shift until I could leave the store. Pretending to be fine and not cry during the ride home with Auntie was torturous.

Thankfully, she was also distracted. Once home, I sunk in my bed and curled up like a shrimp in the middle of my bed. I didn't change my clothes, wash my face, or brush my teeth.

"Please help me through this, my Lord, God and heaven. Please help me. Why did he? How could he?" I cried until sleep took me.

The next few days were difficult, but I managed to keep a smile on at school. I had become an expert at pretending even on the worst days. A week later Alex called . . . and the following days, but I had nothing to say. I saw him again at our dance show—he came as Chloe's date, his eyes filled with pain and unexpressed emotions. I didn't say a word. The first stab was enough, and here he was with Chloe for the final kill. I was stunned, disappointed, but nothing like the first incident. Chloe and I used to call each other best friends and she knew how I felt about Alex. There would be no reconciliation between Alex and I after this. I wished them happiness.

We were invited to my father's for the holidays, but Uncle excused us by saying he had to work. I suspected he didn't even ask for the time off. He worked every day, overtime, and holidays, and Auntie went back to school for her master's degree.

Tori was busy with work and her fiancé, Eric, with whom she was expecting their first child, a baby girl, in a few months. She was thrilled, but uncomfortable with toting a large belly. Uncle David teased her about how much she hated bananas before pregnancy, but now she ate them constantly. Tori and Eric were always talking about their plans together to move out, but they fought constantly, and it just never happened. Tori didn't graduate from high school, but her aunt Suzanne helped her get a job driving for the school district with a good income and a flexible schedule. Auntie and Uncle were eager to have a baby in the house and catered to Tori's every whim.

For a time, our home was revived with a splash of hope and happiness with the baby's pending arrival. As a pastor, Uncle would have preferred that Tori was a little older and married, but he didn't care as much for Eric as he did for Kamel, so he didn't push the issue. He still mentioned hopes of Tori and Kamel getting back together . . . with Tori anything was possible.

The Gift of Love

C hristmastime proved to be much more difficult than I had expected since everywhere I looked, everyone was paired up as a couple. On Christmas Day I was especially low, but I tried to focus on the reason for the season, Jesus Christ. I prayed to wish him a happy birthday.

I missed Mom and Ronnie and imagined them celebrating with family, enjoying the loud rattling sounds of cans as cars passed by dragging them, eating lots of candy and pastries and all the delicious food for the festivities.

I thought about Grandma; what would she be doing in heaven? *Do they celebrate, too?*

We exchanged presents early in the morning as usual, but after that, we all scattered to separate rooms. The tension persisted, and we found ways to escape. Auntie and Uncle didn't argue but that just made it feel like a bomb waiting to explode. I already knew there was nothing I could do.

I sat in my room; what do I do next? What were Mom and Ronnie doing? I closed my eyes and imagined. Mom was riding her new motorcycle, Ronnie hugging her tight and screaming in delight along the way. They were on the way to Grandma's to visit for Christmas, but first they stopped by the market to pick up some fruits and candy to give away. Mom was laughing and Ronnie was enjoying delicacies. I inhaled. I could smell the market and the heat from the sun. The sensation awakened me back to reality, bringing tears to my eyes.

I got on my knees and prayed, thankful to God for my life, for survival, for love, the birthdays when I was celebrated by Uncle and Auntie. The pair of white jeans, the white pearl earrings, my Precious Moments Bible. "These are as precious as you are," Auntie had said. I was honored. I didn't have those celebrations with my father—in fact, he thought my birthday was in April, when really it was in March. There were yearly grand parties for the little ones, with lots of food and presents and in the Philippines, a roasted whole pig which was a sign of wealth. A tear rolled down, tickling my cheek, and onto the bed.

I prayed even harder for my family. "Please help them, Father." Truly, I didn't know what to ask for. I didn't know what needed to be fixed.

Soon, I would be on my way to college, independent from all the troubles of home.

I concentrated on thinking about my blessings. I had learned to speak English, graduated high school with honors, been a Miss Teen USA contestant, been chosen district president for the youth of my church organization, made captain of a drill team, been a cheerleader, dance team member, part of an award-winning choir, and was crowned prom queen for my class. The visions of blessings overwhelmed me.

"Why did you choose to bless me, Father?" I asked. I sobbed.

There was nothing I couldn't do with God on my side—He was my protector, redeemer, and comforter, granting me success upon success, when I was called ugly and had no reason to believe in myself. Because of His love and my mom's caring, I tried hard always even when I was scared. I was the miracle of my mother's love—no amount of abuse could ever erase that solid foundation of love. It was in my spirit forever.

"God, what's next?" I asked. "Will I see my mother again?"

I knew in my heart that I would even through the silence all these years with no letter or phone call. But despite everything I had achieved, I knew this was only the beginning.

"God, what's next?" I whispered.

CPSIA information can be obtained
at www.ICGtesting.com
Printed in the USA
FSHW02n1713070818
51081FS

9 781632 135186